QUICK
STRENGTH
FOR
RUNNERS

8 WEEKS **TO A BETTER RUNNER'S BODY**

QUICK STRENGTH FOR RUNNERS

JEFF HOROWITZ

an imprint of Ulysses Press
PO Box 3440
Berkeley, CA 94703
www.velopress.com

Library of Congress Cataloging-in-Publication Data

Horowitz, Jeffrey.
  Quick strength for runners : 8 weeks to a better runner's body / Jeff Horowitz.
    pages cm
  Includes index.
  ISBN 978-1-937715-12-0 (pbk.)
1. Running—Training. 2. Muscle strength—Physiological aspects. I. Title.
  GV1061.5.H67 2013
  796.42—dc23
                        2013029296

Cover design | Kristin Weber
Cover photograph | Bruce Buckley
Interior design | Vicki Hopewell
Composition | Jessica Xavier, Planet X Design
Exercise photography | Bruce Buckley
Hair and makeup | Kris Clark
Additional photos | p. 5, AP Photo/Diether Endlicher; p. 6, AP Photo/Alastair Grant; p. 8, Thinkstock; pp. 36–38, Rugile Kaladyte; p. 199, Brad Kaminski
Illustrations | Charlie Layton

Text set in Vitesse

10 9 8

CONTENTS

Once upon a time, about twenty years ago, to be precise, runners believed that they didn't have to do anything but run.

AMBY BURFOOT
1968 Boston Marathon Champion and former editor of *Runner's World magazine*

INTRODUCTION

Let's start with a bit of honesty: Not all runners love strength training. If you are like most runners, you would rather lace up your trainers and spend time out on a trail or road than work out in a gym. I understand that. You didn't become a runner to spend more time indoors. There is a whole world of routes to explore when you are out on a run, and none of them pass through a weight room.

But you picked up this book anyway. More likely than not, you did so because you realize that doing nothing but running is not working out so well for you.

Maybe this realization came to you during a layoff from running caused by an injury. Estimates of the rate of injury for runners vary widely, but it may be as high as 80 percent for all runners in a given year and 80 percent for each individual runner over the course of his or her lifetime.

Each of these injuries comes at a physical, emotional, and financial cost. An injury may result in a layoff from running ranging from a week to several months and may require X-rays and MRIs, visits to various physicians, and physical therapy.

The anger, frustration, and sense of helplessness that often accompany these injuries are harder to measure. Injured runners may feel betrayed by their own bodies and isolated from their network of running friends. A long layoff may leave runners wondering if being injured and limited is their new permanent reality. These are hard times for such runners. Frustration often leads them to spend thousands of dollars on products and treatments that often promise quick cures but that rarely deliver results.

I remember one period when I was dealing with a debilitating foot problem. After spending six months visiting different specialists and undergoing various therapies, I realized that had a doctor recommended smearing peanut butter on my foot to speed healing, I would have done it. In fact, I would have smeared peanut butter over my entire body just to be doubly sure! I suspect that I am not the only runner who would have been willing to do that. Perhaps you have felt that way yourself.

Or maybe you picked up this book because you have read about how strength training can actually help *prevent* injuries and improve your running. Perhaps you are even doing some strength training already, but you sus-

pect that you could do a better job if you knew a bit more about it.

Whatever led you to be interested in strength training, you have picked up this book, and that's a good thing. Because all those articles and bits of advice were right: Strength training—the *right* kind of strength training—will make you a stronger, more injury-resistant runner.

Examining the "Simple" Act of Running

Of all the world's great sports, running is perhaps the simplest. No referee is needed to administer complicated rules and no scorer is needed to tabulate points. There are no formulas for figuring out who gets into the playoffs because there are no playoffs.

Running generally requires very little equipment, and no dedicated field or court is absolutely necessary. Almost anyone can run almost anywhere, and running is something most people learned to do when they were only two or three years old.

Even racing is breathtakingly simple. All the racers line up and at the signal run from here to there as fast as they can.

And yet the *act* of running is enormously complicated. It requires the balancing of the entire body as it rotates and hurtles through space, the flexion and extension of a long list of joints, and the timed contraction and release of muscles from head to toe.

Consider this: The liftoff phase of your running motion, when you raise up your leg, is itself a complicated choreography of movement. It requires the contraction of the hip flexor muscles along your lower trunk, as well as of the anterior tibialis muscle of your shin and the leg biceps muscles of your rear thigh. Together, these actions produce flexion of your hip and knee joints while positioning your foot in a toes-up position.

For all this to take place, the opposing muscle groups must relax and lengthen in an ordered sequence. The quadriceps muscles in your front thigh, the soleus and gastrocnemius muscles in your calf, and the gluteus maximus muscle in your backside must all engage in a controlled extension.

And that is not all. You are not doing all these movements from a solid, stable position: You are lunging upward and forward as you are getting airborne. As you do this, your central nervous system avoids crashes, falls, sprains, strains, and other calamities by engaging a multitude of other muscles, large and small, to help you maintain balance in space, in a process called "proprioception."

Ready for more? While all these actions are taking place, your brain is ordering your arms to swing in opposition to the movement of your legs, which helps you maintain alignment along your central axis.* If you are running on uneven terrain, such as on an off-road trail, your brain is also ordering quick adjustments with each step to keep you vertical. Ligaments and tendons heave and pull while small muscles contract, hold, and then release. Elsewhere, your body is busy regulating heat, supplying oxygen and fuel, and removing waste products.

All this happens in the simple action of running a single step.

If we were required to consciously control all these actions, we would be hard-pressed to even get out of bed in the morning. And yet with the assistance of our central nervous systems and our networks of muscles, we do. Every day. We learn to run, and many of us start running for hours and then run in long-distance races. But few of us think about the choreography of running and what is required to make it work.

Why is this all so complicated? Because running is an inherently unbalanced activity. It comprises a series of controlled forward falls. And during the process of running, you are never balanced equally on your two legs. Instead, you are on one foot, then up in the air, and then on the other foot. To fully understand these movements and how strength training

---

* This is the vertical line through your body on which your weight is evenly balanced while spinning; imagine your body as a top rotating on a spindle.

relates to running, we need to delve into the biomechanics of running.

Running is, of course, primarily about moving forward. As opposed to other sports, such as basketball or tennis, that involve moving in multiple directions, running basically occurs in a single plane of motion: what exercise physiologists call the "sagittal plane," which divides your body front to back, producing two mirrored images. When you are running, everything moves forward and backward on this plane: One of your arms and the opposite leg swing forward as the opposite two swing backward and vice versa.

Now the really challenging aspect of running occurs to you *laterally* as you run. When you land on one foot, you are in a very unstable position. And what happens at that moment can greatly affect your running and your odds of getting injured.

Try a quick demonstration. Stand on one foot. Now try holding that position for 10 seconds, but with your eyes closed.

How did you do? If you are like most people, you wobbled a bit, and after a few seconds, you found yourself touching down with your upraised foot to keep balanced.

This unsteadiness is caused by the fact that one of your two main supports—your legs—was taken off the ground. Clos-ing your eyes adds to the difficulty by removing the visual cues that your body also uses to maintain balance; when those are gone, standing on one leg is not an easy task.

So what does this have to do with running? In a word, everything.

When you run, you alternate standing briefly on one foot, then the other. At the moment of touchdown, your body struggles to maintain balance because one of its two main supports—your legs—has been removed. Your body will naturally try to center itself on your planted leg. This in turn puts pressure on the muscles of that leg's outer hip—the gluteus medius.* If the gluteus medius cannot hold firm against this pressure, then the hip will collapse outward.

Take a look at the photo on page 5. It shows world marathon record holder Paula Radcliffe in a tough moment at the 2004 Olympic Games in Athens. Having suffered from a leg injury and stomach problems, she had dropped out of the marathon, held just five days before the pictured event, the 10K. Unfortunately for her, she fared no better in this race. Fatigue and continuing stomach problems were plaguing her, and she dropped out of this race as well.

---

* It is tempting to use the common term glutes here, but there are actually several muscles in this group, each of which performs a different task, so we are going to be more specific in our terminology when the movement we are describing requires it, as in this discussion. Otherwise, we will keep things easy and refer to the entire group together as glutes whenever possible.

All this is vividly displayed not only on her face, contorted by effort and discomfort, but also in her form, which has broken down dramatically. Her gluteus medius is no longer able to hold her body's weight as she lands. The photo captures a moment when her right hip has collapsed outward. This in turn causes her left hip to sag. With her hips angled down toward her left, her spine angles to her right. To keep her balance, she compensates by shifting her right shoulder down, which then causes her to tilt her head to the left.

The net result? Paula has contorted herself into an S shape.

Does her form matter? As the great but notoriously awkward-looking Czech Olympic runner Emil Zátopek once said, "I shall learn to have a better style once they start judging races according to their beauty." Emil cared less about his form than he did about finishing first, which he did often. So what is really so important about Paula's form in this photo?

Plenty. When a runner's hip collapses outward, that motion puts strain on that entire area. Specifically, the hip on that side pushes against a thick rope of connective tissue that runs from the point of the hip, called the "ilium," along the outside of the leg, down to a bone in the lower leg called the "tibia." This structure, called the "iliotibial (IT) band," helps stabilize the leg during forward motion. When the IT band is stretched taut, it can rub along the outside

Paula Radcliffe showing signs of distress in the 10K at the 2004 Olympic Games

of the knee, which can lead to inflammation and pain in that area, as well as strain to the lower back as the spine is contorted.

To sum up: Poor hip strength leads to outward collapse of the hip on foot strike, which can lead to strain and tightness in the IT band and pain to the outer part of the knee and the lower back.

Many runners have had this problem at one time or another, but few understand the mechanics that led to the problem. Instead, they react by treating the symptoms: They stretch the IT band in an effort to gently loosen it and thereby prevent rubbing at their knee, which would reduce irritation and inflammation in the knee. Then they apply ice to the knee and take anti-inflammatories to further reduce pain and swelling in that area. Those strategies will help, but only momentarily. The real problem, as we now know, is not in the IT band or the knee; it is in the hip.

This problem is easy to spot. In action, runners who have collapsing hips have a noticeable hip sway as one hip and then the other falls outward. The hems of their shirts pitch and roll like a ship on rough seas, and if the runner has a ponytail, it will swing from side to side like the wag of a dog's tail.

Now look at the photo of Paula on the right, which was taken almost exactly one year after her disaster at the Athens Olympics. She is running in the 2005 Track and Field World Championships in Helsinki, and she is on her way to winning the gold medal in the marathon in a championship record time of 2:20:57.

In this second photo Paula is engaged in lifting her knee, but we can see that on the side where she just had her foot planted—

her right side—the gluteus medius muscle was able to keep her right side straight. This forces her hip girdle into proper position, which causes her unweighted left hip to elevate as she raises her left knee.

Paula Radcliffe running the marathon like a champion in 2005

The result? If you dropped a plumb line from her shoulder to the ground, you would see how perfectly straight she is. The elevation of her unweighted hip is a classic indicator of perfect form. Similarly, if you held a level across her shoulders, you would find them to be quite nearly parallel to the ground. Without the need to compensate for any unwanted lateral movement and dropping hips, Paula is able to hold her spine straighter and her head higher than she had in Athens, swing her arms smoothly and efficiently, and run fast.

Put directly, Paula in the photo on page 5 has a higher risk of injury than Paula in the photo on page 6.

Could strength training have helped with this? Absolutely. Paula's problems in Athens had a lot to do with challenges she faced in training while preparing for those Games, but in most cases when runners who have a similar breakdown in their form strengthen their gluteus medius muscles, they improve their ability to stay in alignment. This helps them avoid strain to their IT bands and all the other negative consequences that follow.

The Case for Strength Training

Imagine that you have been feeling a twinge in your right hamstring muscles. It started with a bit of soreness when you first began running, but recently that muscle group has been taking longer and longer to

ease up, and now you are feeling some pain in that area nearly all the time. You react by stretching your hamstrings and applying ice and heat to the affected area. Not a bad strategy, but the injury is not really getting any better. This may be because you are addressing the wrong problem.

As we discussed, the act of running requires the activation of a number of large and small muscles in ordered sequence. The part of the running motion that involves push-off and knee flexion is called the "toe-off, or pawing, phase." Imagine a lion scraping at the ground with its paw; that's you as you push against the ground to shove your body forward.

The major muscle groups involved in this motion are the hamstrings (comprising three on each side), which govern knee contraction, and the gluteus maximus muscles of your backside, which control hip extension. These are some of the most powerful muscles in your body, and for you to run properly, they must be fully engaged.

To get an idea of how this works, stand facing a wall. Put your left hand against the wall for balance, and place your right hand on your backside. Now swing your right leg backward, being sure to keep your knee locked. As you do this, you will feel your gluteus maximus muscle on your right backside contract and bunch up as it draws your leg backward.

This is the movement that initiates

the pawing-off phase of running. The contraction of your hamstrings occurs quickly afterward as you follow though with your movement.

The photo below shows what this phase looks like in action. The hip on the right side is extended, pulled back by the gluteus muscles on that side. The right hamstring muscles are also engaged, which has caused the knee to bend. This is what running looks like when those muscles are working properly.

But let's get back to your tweaky hamstring. Could it be that your gluteus maximus muscle is not powerful enough to do what you are asking of it while running?

Hip extension and glutes contraction shown in action on the road

If that is the case, then the burden of work falls on your hamstrings. But your hamstrings are not strong enough to do all the work, and they eventually are overwhelmed by the effort and begin to break down quicker than they can recover. This could have been the cause of the pain and inflammation you are feeling on your right side.

Weakness in the gluteus maximus can be addressed with strength training; just running will not directly strengthen those muscles. Why? Because the gluteus maximus muscles are already failing to fire properly. Running more will not engage them any more effectively; that will only continue to stress the hamstring muscles, possibly leading to an even more serious injury, such as a rupture.

In sum, the complex motion of running requires balanced strength throughout the body—not just in the obvious running muscles such as the hamstrings and the glutes, which power forward motion, but also in a host of stabilizing muscles throughout the body. Put another way, to improve as a runner, you need to run. But if all you do is run, you may not be running for long.

Common Myths About Strength Training

So now that you have a better idea of how running mechanics work, and how building strength can help you avoid injury and keep you running into the future, are you willing to commit to adding strength training to your routine?

Before you answer, let's review some common concerns about strength training, as well as a few myths that often scare people away.

MYTH: Strength training will make me bigger, and I do not want to be bigger.

Strength training can enlarge your muscles—known as "hypertrophy"—but that is not an inevitable outcome of strength training. Think of doing strength training as using a tool: It will do what you ask of it. If you ask it to build muscle mass, it will do so. But if instead you ask it to build only lean muscle without adding mass, it will do that instead. The key is in *how* you strength-train.

Generally speaking, if you work against greater resistance for fewer repetitions of an exercise, you will encourage hypertrophy. Conversely, if you keep resistance moderate and perform a high number of repetitions of each exercise, you will improve strength and muscle endurance without experiencing a significant improvement in muscle size.* The choice is yours.

The strength training plan presented here is not focused on building muscle mass. In these pages you will not find such bodybuilding staples as heavy bench presses or dumbbell rows. In fact, you could have an entire strength training session without picking up a single weight.

Keep in mind, too, that you are naturally limited by your genetics and body type. If you are a lean runner who has always had difficulty gaining weight, you might not be able to put on much muscle mass even if you wanted to. The odds of you getting bulky accidentally while following a runner's strength training plan are very low.

But what if you tend to put on weight easily? Should you avoid strength training altogether? Certainly not. That would be like throwing away the baby with the bathwater. The smarter approach is to structure your strength workouts to emphasize high-repetition exercises.

As an added benefit, the research increasingly shows that relatively low-resistance strength training—the kind we are going to be talking about here—can lead to significant improvements in cardiovascular fitness. That means targeted

---

* There is some research suggesting that gains in muscle mass can be achieved with lower-resistance training, but only in the context of greater total workout volume. The research did not look at introducing different modes of training, such as unstable complex movements, as opposed to standard weight-lifting exercises. See R. Ogasawara et al., "Low-Load Bench Press Training to Fatigue Results in Muscle Hypertrophy Similar to High-Load Bench Press Training," *International Journal of Clinical Medicine* 4 (February 2013): 114–121, doi:10.4236/ijcm.2013.42022; and N. A. Burd et al., "Low-Load High Volume Resistance Exercise Stimulates Muscle Protein Synthesis More Than High-Load Low-Volume Resistance Exercise in Young Men," *PLoS ONE* 5(8) (2010): e12033, doi:10.1371/journal.pone.0012033.

strength training can help improve your form and your endurance.*

MYTH: *Strength training will make me less flexible.*

Athletes who have inelastic, overdeveloped muscles, are usually described as "muscle-bound." They are characterized as being rigid and inflexible. This label is often applied to weight lifters and bodybuilders and is cited by wary athletes who avoid strength training because they do not want to become inflexible.

This is a myth.

It is simply not true that strength training leads to shortening of tendons and ligaments or loss in their pliability.

The truth is that an athlete either stretches and is flexible or isn't. Strength training will not dictate flexibility one way or the other. This is certainly true of the program presented here, which, as we just discussed, is not designed to lead to big increases in muscle mass.

MYTH: *I will have to go to a gym and use barbells and machines.*

Those modes of training can certainly be effective, but there is more than one way to skin a cat. You do not need to join a gym and use machines in order to strength-

train. With a minimal amount of equipment, you can do everything you need to do almost anywhere you choose to do it.

MYTH: *Strength training will take up too much time.*

When I do presentations on strength training to large groups of runners, I start by asking, how many people had a running injury over the previous year? A forest of hands go up. I then ask, how many injuries involved a layoff of at least a week? Most hands stay up. A month? A lot of hands remain in the air. Three months or more? Some hands are still up.

Then I pose this question: If you could have avoided the injury by spending just 15–20 minutes, 2–3 times a week, doing strength work in your own home, would you have been willing to do it?

For most of us, taking up strength training is a no-brainer when we look at it this way. In the long run, strength training will give you more time to hit the roads, not less, and that is exactly what this book will provide. By following the structured workout plan presented here, you can fit all the strength training you need to do into a minimal amount of time and also avoid the injuries that are responsible for the real disruptions to your workout schedule.

---

* J. Steele et al., "Resistance Training to Momentary Muscular Failure Improves Cardiovascular Fitness in Humans: A Review of Acute Physiological Responses and Chronic Physiological Adaptation," *Journal of Exercise Physiology Online*, 15(3) (June 2012): 53–80.

MYTH: *Muscle turns to fat if you stop lifting weights.*

This is a persistent misconception supported by many examples of former weight lifters who have gotten fat after they stopped working out. But this conclusion mistakes coincidence with causality. Muscle can no more turn into fat than lead can turn into gold. They are different types of tissue. But if you get in the habit of eating more to support the extra calorie burn that strength training provides and then fail to dial back the eating when you stop strength training, those extra calories will be stored as fat, not because you stopped strength training, but because you're taking in more calories than you are using.

MYTH: *Strength training is not for women.*

Obviously, this myth applies to only half the population, and fortunately it is a myth that is rapidly dying out. It wasn't that long ago that women were considered physically unable to compete in long distance running, and that strength training was considered "unladylike."

Today, that view has been largely replaced by acceptance and encouragement of female participation in sport, prompted in large part by the enactment in 1972 of federal legislation barring sex-ual discrimination in any higher education program that receives federal financial assistance, known colloquially by its chapter heading, Title IX.*

Nevertheless, for that minority of people who still believe that sweating and grunting and pushing for athletic excellence is something suited only for men, they need only take a quick glance at the women who are participating on pro sports teams, at women's Olympic achievements, and at their road racing success to become convinced that there is nothing unfeminine about striving for athletic excellence.

How to Use This Book

The purpose of this book is to take the guesswork out of strength training and present it in a way that any runner can immediately put to use. The chapters that follow will provide you with the knowledge and direction to implement your own progressive strength training plan. Just follow each workout as written and illustrated; it will be like having a personal strength coach come to your home twice a week.

We will begin with an overview of strength training generally and then look at it specifically in regard to runners. We will discuss the equipment that you will

---

* Title IX is a portion of the Education Amendments of 1972, Public Law No. 92-318, 86 Stat. 235 (June 23, 1972), codified at 20 U.S.C., sec. 1681-1688.

need to get started and the types of exercises that you will be doing.

Next, we will review each exercise in detail, explaining why you are doing it, as well as offering options on how to make it more challenging—and effective—once you have mastered the basic form.

Finally, you will be presented with an 8-week detailed training plan that will place these exercises in a progressively more difficult format, challenging you a bit more each week as you build toward your target: improved running form, strength, and overall health.

By the end of the book, you will be able to continue using the program as presented or to make your own program based on the principles articulated here. Ultimately, following this program will not only make you a better runner; it will also leave you better prepared for that other great activity: life.

The only remaining question is *when* to start this program. If you have a target race on your calendar, start your strength training 9 weeks before the race. This leaves the last week before the race open for resting and tapering. The benefit of choosing this option is that you can put your new strength to work for you when you want it most; the strength that you build during your race preparation will quickly enable you to run better in training and racing.

Another option is to start this program during your off-season, after you have run your goal race. Since most off-season training plans involve a step back in training volume and intensity for a month or so after the goal race is run, the off-season is an ideal moment in your schedule to devote a little time and effort to adding something new to your training routine. Also, having just come through a training cycle and race, you might be a little burned out from your usual routine. Implementing a strength training program could be exactly the kind of change that you are looking for to reenergize your workouts.

The final and perhaps best option is to simply start the program now, regardless of where you are in your running schedule. Remember, the sooner you start the program, the sooner you will begin to reap the benefits, so there is no time like the present to get started.

Before we get the details of the program, though, think a moment about your commitment to strength training. The program presented here should not be just about getting a quick fix for a nagging injury. To run strong and stay healthy, you must commit to making strength training part of your regular routine. Many runners who begin a strength training routine at some point after suffering an injury drop it once their hurt body heals and their memories of desperation and despair fade. Or when they are pressed for time and struggling to squeeze in their regular run, they begin to skip a strength training workout here and there, and soon they stop doing strength training altogether.

In a way, all of that makes sense. Running is a priority and passion for all of us. It lifts our mood, sparks our creativity, leaves us feeling more alive than at any other time of the day, and opens the world up to us. In comparison, there is no strength training plan in existence that can generate these results.

Luckily, the goal here is not to replace running with strength training or even give strength training equal billing in your training schedule. The aim is to include strength training *somewhere* in your busy schedule, on a consistent basis, a few times a week. This is simply the best way to recover from an injury *and* help ensure that you will not be sidelined by a debilitating running injury again.

1
STRENGTH TRAINING FOR RUNNERS:
A PRIMER

Before we can outline a workout, we have to be sure that we are talking the same language. Many terms get tossed around in articles and books about strength training, but these terms may mean different things to different people. To ensure that we are all on the same page, let's start with some definitions.

Strength training is a method of improving muscular strength by gradually increasing the body's ability to resist force through the use of free weights, machines, or a person's own body weight.

Strength training workouts are designed to impose increasingly greater resistance against the body's movement in one or more planes, which in turn stimulates development of muscle strength to meet the added demand. These workouts consist of short, repeated bursts of activity that target one or more specific muscles and are separated by rest (or a shift to an exercise that works a different muscle or muscle group, as is the case in our workouts).

The thinking must be done first,
before the training begins.

PETER COE
Father and coach to Olympian Sebastian Coe,
former world record holder in the 800 meters, mile, and 1,500 meters

Each **exercise** within a workout targets one or more muscle groups through the performance of a given movement that puts stress on those muscles.

A **repetition,** or **rep,** is the performance of a single exercise, from the starting position, through the movement, and back to the start again.

A **set** is the continuous performance of a given number of repetitions.

The performance of strength training creates a **stimulus** to the body, which triggers a **stimulus response.** This is the magic of all training, including running: When we put a reasonable but challenging burden on the body (a stimulus), we create minor damage to the muscle cells. The body responds by repairing that damage in a way that makes it more capable of successfully handling that stress in the future (a stimulus response, or adaptation). This process is known as the **overload** approach to exercise.

When done correctly, this kind of workout routine will, over time, prompt the body to become stronger and fitter. However, if the stimulus is greater than the body's ability to respond, the body will simply break down, resulting in injury. Keeping the stimulus at an appropriate level, therefore, is the trick.

As you will see in the chapter on specific exercises, we will moderate the stimulus by becoming familiar with various forms of each exercise. In this way, we do not have to start with a very difficult form of a new exercise and we can make each exercise more difficult as the body adapts to the stimulus that the basic form presented.

Different kinds of stimulus generally trigger different kinds of adaptations by the body. We touched on this subject in the Introduction when we addressed the myth that all strength training will lead to big gains in muscle mass. If the stimulus involves high amounts of resistance performed near maximum capacity for a limited number of reps—say, 1–6 reps per set—that may be true. But if the stimulus involves relatively low resistance and a higher number of reps—say, 14–20—then improved muscle tone and endurance can be expected and significant addition of mass is unlikely. This latter approach is the one that we will be aiming for.

It's All About Performance

When most people think of strength training, they probably imagine bodybuilders pumping iron or working their way through rows of machines with stacks of plates attached by cables to pulleys and handles.

This presumption is not wrong, but it does not represent the only types of strength training available. In fact, we are generally going to steer away from those. Here's why: Those exercises isolate muscle groups from the rest of your body and,

CROSSTRAINING VERSUS STRENGTH TRAINING

Strength training increases the power in specific muscles and muscle groups. This kind of exercise is fueled by a compound stored within the muscle cells called adenosine triphosphate, which can be processed by the body without the presence of oxygen. For that reason, this type of exercise is called *anaerobic*. Because it does not tax the cardiovascular system, strength training will not significantly improve cardiovascular fitness.

Crosstraining generally involves incorporating different modes of cardiovascular exercise, such as swimming or cycling, into a routine as a substitute for running. This kind of training can be very beneficial, especially if it is low-impact or nonimpact exercise, because it saves wear and tear on joints and tendons. In the case of cycling, it also helps strengthen other muscle groups that support running, such as the quadriceps.

But crosstraining is not really strength training. Although different crosstraining routines will train various muscle groups, the main impact is on improving the efficiency and capacity of the cardiovascular system, not on building significant strength in those muscle groups—especially in the stabilizing muscles that control lateral movement.

even though they are effective in strengthening muscles in a particular way, they do not teach your body how to move in ways that improve you as a runner.

Our aim here is not just to work the muscle but also to work the *movement*. Every runner I have ever met, whether a back-of-the-pack runner or an elite racer, has wanted to know how to get faster. Just looking good is usually not on the top of the list; runners are usually more concerned with performance than aesthetics.

Improving performance, then, is our main priority. This goal will guide all our exercise choices and will make this program different from many other strength workouts. For people who have experience already with strength training, this might bring some surprises.

Consider the Bench Press. In this exercise (shown on page 18), a person lies on a weight lifting bench and grips a barbell that is resting above him or her on two support arms. The exerciser lifts the bar up off the supports, lowers it to the chest, and then presses the weight back up in the air to the starting position. When the set is complete, the exerciser replaces the bar onto the bench's support arms.

The Bench Press is considered a staple of a standard weight lifting routine, and I have nothing bad to say about it. But let's look at exactly what it does for you and what it does *not* do.

A Bench Press involves engaging the pectoral muscles of the chest, the deltoid muscles of the shoulders, and the triceps muscles of the upper arms to extend the shoulder and elbow joints in order to push the barbell up and away from the body. Because it engages a range of joints and muscles, the Bench Press is considered a complex movement and has a relatively big impact on the body. Also, because it involves balancing weight in the air, it is referred to as an "open-chain" exercise, which engages the targeted muscles in an even more effective way as they struggle to hold the barbell steady. This makes the Bench Press an especially effective exercise for building strength and fitness.

All of that is great—unless you are a runner, in which case it does not really mean that much to you.

The Bench Press

For starters, the Bench Press emphasizes a movement that you will never use during running and racing: pushing something heavy away from your body.

Second, while those upper body muscles are getting a workout, the lower body remains fairly passive. The feet rest on the floor, and the abdominal muscles are relatively relaxed. From the waist up, the exercise might be a struggle for survival, but from the waist down, it is a day at the beach. None of the core muscles that are so important to running are being used.

Consider a similar movement: the Push-Up. There is nothing high tech or cutting edge about this one; it is more or less the same exercise you did in PE class back in middle school, though perhaps now with better form.

Because the hands are on the floor during a Push-Up, it is classified as a "closed-chain" exercise and involves no balancing of weights. In fact, no weights are involved at all. Although there are ways in which the exercise can be made more difficult, there are limits to what can be done. The resistance load simply cannot be increased as much as it can on a machine or barbell. That is a drawback because the adaptation stimulus cannot be increased by as much as the body may be able to handle—especially if the desired result is a dramatic improvement in strength and muscle mass.

But let's look closer at this exercise. Even though the muscles of the upper body

The Push-Up

are not getting as much of a workout here as they might from doing the Bench Press, at least the muscles of the lower body are finally getting engaged. The muscles of the hips, abdominals, and lower back are all straining to keep the body rigid during the movement. Because these are the muscles that we will be relying on during running, the Push-Up is a better exercise for runners than the Bench Press.

With this in mind, let's move on to discuss the three different types of strength training that this book will focus on: balance, core strength, and run-specific strength. These are the three areas of fitness that have the most impact on runners as they move through the unstable portions of the running motion.

Balance work strengthens the neural pathways that trigger key muscles needed to keep you upright and in proper position. Core strength gives your body the ability to maintain the proper position that running requires. And run-specific strength trains the muscles that are directly used in running to respond more forcefully and

effectively when your brain directs them to move while running.

Balance

As mentioned earlier, the body governs itself in space using a form of muscle control known as **proprioception.** When your body finds itself thrown off balance, such as when the road you are running on is slanted or you step on a rock while running, a network of nerves and muscles fires to make tiny adjustments in order to keep you from finding yourself on the seat of your pants.

To improve proprioception, we have to challenge the body to balance itself in a number of different ways. Examples of these kinds of exercises include doing movements while standing on one leg or while standing on an unstable base. Although the movements themselves may not necessarily target the feet and ankles, they will nevertheless be getting a good workout during each of the exercises in this section. To confirm this for yourself, look in a mirror while exercising. You will likely see the muscles of the shins—the anterior tibialis—twitch as they struggle to maintain balance.

Ultimately, training to enhance balance is not just good for running; it is also a good habit to maintain throughout life so that you can remain highly functional. Losing balance as we age and suffering crippling falls are not inevitable. If we train to stay fit and active, then we can be strong and healthy in our later years.*

Core Strength

Working the core seems to be all the rage in fitness, and for good reason, but many people have an incomplete idea about what this means.

A strong core involves more than having a beach-ready six-pack. Having strong abdominal muscles is certainly part of it, but core strength involves something much greater: power in all the muscles from the midthigh to the lower ribcage, on the front, back, and sides of the body. This includes the muscles of the hips and lower back.

Why is the core so important? As demonstrated in the photos of Paula Radcliffe in the Introduction, good form depends on having balanced strength in the muscle groups that hold the body stable while running. If your foundation is weak, then every movement of your arms and legs will pull your body off-line, which in turn makes you less efficient and can stress other muscle groups, leaving them open to injury. A strong core avoids these problems by providing you with a solid base.

When I think of the core, I am often reminded of those excavators that dig trenches at construction sites. Past the long boom arm with its bucket, down near the wheels, there is usually a pair of stabilizing arms that are lowered from the body of the vehicle down to the ground. These arms keep the base steady as the boom arm reaches out to move loads of earth.

Having core strength is like having a pair of stabilizers attached to your body, holding you steady against the ground. No matter what your limbs might be doing, you can trust your core to keep things under control.

For me, this once became a matter of life and death. While competing in a long-course cycling event in 2012, I found myself hurtling down a hill on a poorly maintained road. As my bike rattled over broken asphalt, it hit a certain frequency of vibration that left it harder and harder to

---

* Research has demonstrated that older individuals make gains in both balance and force production when they follow a program that incorporates both balance and resistance exercises. See L. Wolfson, R. Whipple, C. Derby et al., "Balance and Strength Training in Older Adults: Intervention Gains and Tai Chi Maintenance," *Journal of the American Geriatrics Society* 44 (1996): 498–506.

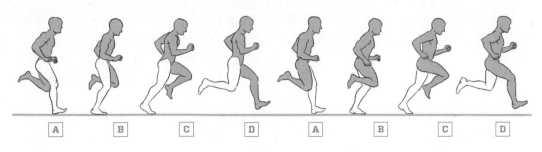

The phases of running, from the right leg to the left

handle. As I struggled with the bike, I saw that I was heading toward a turn banked by a steel barrier. Beyond the barrier was a sharp drop-off through dense woods. As I hurtled toward the barrier at 35 mph, all I could think was, *This is going to be bad.*

I knew that I needed to get the bike under control, but how? I could not just squeeze the brakes at that point; at the speed I was going, that would have been like throwing gasoline on a fire. My wheels probably would have lost their grip on the road and sent me skidding sideways. My only real option, as I saw it, was to clamp down with my body and stop the bike from shaking. I locked my core hard, gripped the bike tightly with my hands and legs, and hoped for the best.

Little by little, the vibrating quieted, and I was able to start slowing the bike. As I rounded the corner, I finally took a deep breath and continued the race.

I am not saying that doing core work may save your life someday. But I am not saying that it won't.

Run-Specific Strength

Improving balance and core strength will undoubtedly help your running. But the final piece that we need to add to our routines are those exercises that directly target the muscles used in running.

Running can appear seamless when done correctly, but exercise physiologists break it down into specific phases (illustrated above):

A **The foot contact phase.** This occurs from the moment when your heel makes contact until your body's full weight is rested on your foot.

B **The midfoot loading phase.** Also known as the propulsion phase, this occurs with full weighting of your foot through extension of your ankle (known as plantar flexion) and the beginning of push-off.

C **The toe-off phase.** This occurs when your heel leaves the ground and your toes push off as your body moves forward.

D **The swing phase.** Also known as the float or recovery phase, this occurs from the moment your toe leaves the ground behind you until your heel touches down below you.

Exercises that target each of these specific phases work to both strengthen the muscles involved in each and imprint correct form on the neurons involved. These exercises are practice for running rather than running itself. They differ from actual running in the same way that practicing free throws differs from playing a game of basketball.

Even though there may be some overlap among these groups, each hits a different fitness target and each will contribute differently to the overall goal of improved running form and speed.

The Body

Any book about strength training is going to include some illustrations of anatomy and muscle groups, and this book is no different. However, instead of beginning with an identification of individual muscles, we are going to talk instead about how all the parts work together and how that shapes the workout routines.

Let's begin by agreeing on how we are going to think about the body. Most athletes think of the body as a collection of parts—the biceps, the pectorals, the del-

toids, and so on—and they focus on how to improve strength in each part.

There is nothing inherently wrong with that approach, but it is a little like thinking of your dinner as a collection of ingredients instead of as a single complex meal. More importantly, this is not how your body thinks of itself.

Sound confusing? Let me explain.

Imagine that your body is a separate entity that you share space with, like a roommate. Just as another person might approach problems and challenges differently from you, so, too, does your body have its own way of handling challenges. Sometimes your body's choices conflict with your own choices, and a battle of wills takes place.

Most of our bodily processes are handled without the control, or even consent, of our conscious minds. Blood pressure, sweat rate, and immune function are all handled by our autonomous nervous systems. This is a good thing. In evolutionary terms, it has left our conscious minds free to make the bigger decisions—like what animal to stalk for dinner or what college to attend—that brought us as a species to the top of the food chain.

In terms of exercise and fitness, our bodies generally take a different view of movement than we do. Our bodies tend to be **inclusive** in performing exercises, whereas strength training tends to be **isolationist**. This can lead to dramatically different ways of performing exercises and can mean the difference between hitting your fitness goals or getting injured.

Let's look at an example. When you pick up a barbell to perform Biceps Curls, you do not really care at all about the weight; you just want to do what you need to do to get stronger and perhaps to get bigger arms. As reaching your goal involves lifting that bar, you will do it.

Your body does not understand this approach. Oddly enough, your body believes that when you pick up a barbell, you are primarily interested in getting that bar off the ground. Your body is essentially very practical, and it believes that you are, too. When you do something, your body will assume that you have got a very good reason to do it, some reason that might mean the difference between eating or being eaten.

Because lifting that bar seems to be a priority for you, your body will aim to do it in the most efficient, effective, orderly way possible. That means using not just your arms to get the bar moving, but also as many muscles as possible, including in your legs and back. If possible, your body will also swing the weight to generate some helpful momentum.

Unfortunately, that is not the proper way to perform this exercise. A Barbell Curl involves elbow flexion only; the rest of the body is supposed to be held rigid while the biceps do all the work. This puts most of the stress on the biceps, which will lead to their improvement.

However, if instead you swing your body and scoop up the bar to raise it up in the air, you will reduce the stress on the biceps. Your body thinks this is good because raising the bar is then easier. But given that you intended to stress the biceps, you will not be achieving your goal and get all the expected results if your body has its way. Worse, you might be compromising other muscle groups, such as those in your lower back, which could cause them injury.

There is a name in strength training for what your body is trying to do: cheating. When you see a person lifting his backside off a bench while doing a Bench Press, or swinging his body while doing Pull-Ups, he is abandoning proper form in favor of a "by any means possible" approach.

When a weight lifter cheats during strength training, she is doing one of three things: trying to involve as many muscle groups as possible to perform the movement, sometimes by changing the angle or position of her body; attempting to generate momentum by swinging her body and the weight; or engaging in a combination of the two.

Weight lifters who cheat while exercising may not be consciously thinking of their movements in this way ("I'm going to change the angle of the exercise to get more leverage by lifting my hips off the bench while doing a Bench Press"). They just naturally end up doing so because it is easier. Experienced, disciplined athletes know not to put form ahead of weight when exercising, so they will not lift a heavier weight than they can handle. Still, this is not the kind of movement the body had in mind.

The body views the muscles as a team. To function well, all the members of the team must work together. Practicing alone will not help team members very much. How effectively can a quarterback practice for game day if he does not have a receiver to throw to? If the aim of practice is to prepare the team to score more points in the game, then practicing together as a team makes a lot more sense than working only on individual movements.

As runners, we should adopt this team concept. Instead of building up strength as an end in itself, we will aim to improve the body's ability to generate power while running. To adopt an old coaching phrase that we referred to earlier in this chapter, we are going to work the *movement*, not just the *muscle*.

By doing this, we enter into a partnership with the body and work with it instead of against it. The effect of this will be apparent almost immediately. Even though many of the exercises contained in this book will be difficult, none should feel as artificial as many other traditional weight lifting movements.

For example, perhaps you are familiar with the Lat Pull-Down, an exercise for the upper back. It is sort of like a Pull-Up, but instead of moving your body against a stationary bar, you keep your body still and pull the bar down to your body. For many people, this is an uncomfortable, awkward movement.

Most of the movements that you will be doing in the workouts in this book will feel relatively comfortable because these movements generally involve challenging your body in a way that feels comfortable and familiar, even when they are difficult. We accomplish this by making sure the exercises follow two basic principles as much as possible: keeping the exercises complex and destabilizing the body.

Keeping the Exercises Complex

An isolation exercise usually involves just one or two joints flexing and extending. In the case of a Biceps Curl, for instance, only one joint—the elbow—is actively being used. This makes the Biceps Curl a **simple movement**. Only the muscles involved in bending and extending the elbow are used in that movement. Even though that is a great workout for the biceps, no other muscles are actively engaged during the exercise, so that Biceps Curl will have a relatively low impact on overall health and athletic performance.

Any exercise that involves using two or more joints is called a **complex movement** because a greater number of muscles are recruited to accomplish the action. A complex exercise is more efficient than a simple exercise in building overall fitness because it engages and challenges more muscle groups. Also, a complex exercise forces the body to coordinate its movements to accomplish the desired result—that is, to learn to play like a team for that movement.

Because the benefits of engaging in complex movements are more in line with the fitness goals we have identified, we are going to put complex movements at the top of our go-to exercise list. Whenever possible, we are going to get as many different joints—and their attendant muscles—involved in a given exercise.

Sometimes this will take the form of a single exercise, but other times it will involve combining two separate exercises into a single, continuous movement. As you work your way through the exercises, think about ways in which you might be able to create your own exercises or combinations—and remember, if you create an exercise, you can name it!

Destabilizing the Body

Muscles may be engaged not only actively, as when a joint is flexed or extended, but also passively, as when a pose is being held. The Push-Up, for example, engages the muscles of the core without extending or contracting them; they work just by holding the body rigid as the upper body completes the exercise.

Forcing the body to balance, then, forces a variety of muscle groups to get engaged and work to accomplish the underlying movement. Or, as we like to say, to work together as a team. This is true even if the target exercise involves a simple movement because while only a single joint might be actively engaged, that is not the full and complete story about what the body is doing.

To get the biggest fitness impact from an exercise, we are going to figure out ways in which we can add instability to as many exercises as possible. As you will soon see, there are many ways to do this:

- We can remove a support by standing on one leg while doing an exercise. This creates lateral instability and forces the muscles of the hips, legs, and core to engage to keep us from toppling over.

- We can sit or lie back on a stability ball while exercising, which forces the core to engage in order to keep us from tipping over.

- Instead of doing exercises with dumbbells bilaterally (a dumbbell in each hand), we can do them unilaterally (a dumbbell in one hand only). This puts lateral pressure on the body as our center of gravity shifts toward the hand with the dumbbell. Think of that scene from *The Flintstones* when a rack of dino-ribs is delivered to their car at a drive-in. Remember what happened? The weight of the ribs flipped the car over. To avoid that same result, the body must engage the core to remain in place.

The net result of all these efforts is to engage more muscles during each exercise and to ask the body to figure out how to control itself in space while moving in complex ways. By challenging the body to figure out the best ways to do this, and to gain strength in order to do it, we will be preparing the body to more effectively and efficiently engage these same muscle groups in the activity we most care about: running.

The Key Muscle Groups

In order to effectively perform the exercises in this training program, you need to have good body awareness. This means having the ability to identify individual muscles and to actively engage them.

In anatomy texts, any discussion of skeletal muscle would include an illustration of a man or woman standing with one arm up, body flayed of skin to reveal the tissue beneath. Individual muscles would be identified with markers and arrows.

By now you know that I like to look at the body a little differently. Instead of simply identifying muscles, we are going to look at them in groups. This will give us an idea of how the body uses them in concert to perform essential movements.

The Push Muscles

These are the muscles that help you thrust something away from you, whether a basketball, a barbell, or a sumo wrestler. The major joints involved are the shoulder and elbow, which will be extended as you push.

Pectorals (Pecs): These are the big muscles of the chest. Made up of the pectoralis major and the underlying pectoralis minor, these bring the shoulder and arm forward when they are contracted.

Deltoids (Delts): These are the muscles of the shoulder. Made up of three muscle groups, they are responsible for forward arm motion (anterior deltoids), lateral arm movement (medial deltoids), and rearward arm movement (posterior deltoid). The medial deltoid is the group that is mostly involved in pushing movements.*

---

* Underneath the delts, and not visible in the illustration here, are the four muscles that make up the rotator cuff. These muscles are responsible for rotating the arm forward and backward.

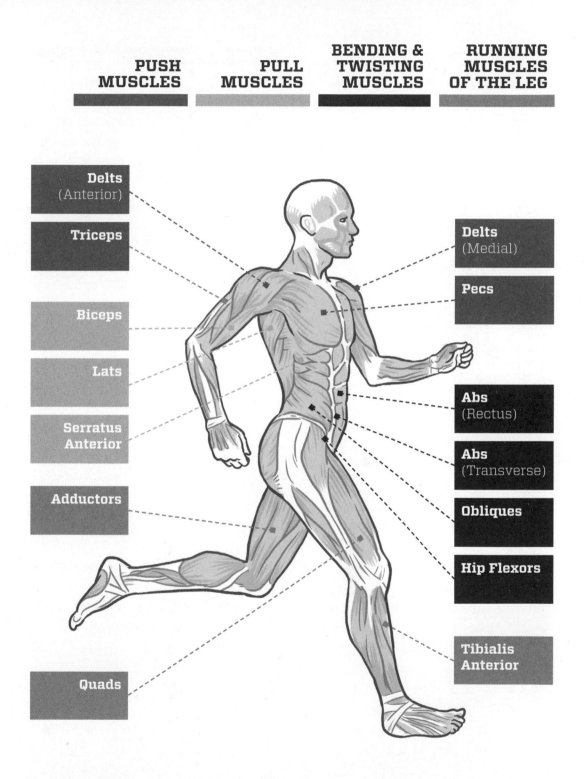

PUSH MUSCLES
PULL MUSCLES
BENDING & TWISTING MUSCLES
RUNNING MUSCLES OF THE LEG

Delts (Anterior)

Triceps

Biceps

Lats

Serratus Anterior

Adductors

Quads

Delts (Medial)

Pecs

Abs (Rectus)

Abs (Transverse)

Obliques

Hip Flexors

Tibialis Anterior

Triceps: This is the muscle located on the back of each upper arm. When it contracts, it forces the arm to straighten out.

The Pull Muscles

These are the muscles that enable you to pull something toward you or you toward it. The major joints involved are the shoulder and elbow, although this time they will be flexed in order to accomplish this movement.

Latissimus Dorsi (Lats): These are the big muscles of the upper back that form a V. They flare out from the spine and are engaged whenever you pull downward from above (or pull your body upward) or pull something directly toward you.

Rhomboids: These are muscles found in the upper midback, inward from the shoulder blades. They help bring the shoulder blades together.

Trapezius (Traps): This is a set of large muscles that flare out from the spine, forming a large diamond shape of muscle. Along with the rhomboids, they help pull the shoulder blades together.

Biceps: This is the muscle at the front of the upper arm. It bends the elbow.

The Bending and Twisting Muscles

These are the muscles, mentioned earlier, collectively known as the **core.** The core is defined as all the muscles from the midthigh to the bottom of the ribcage, 360 degrees around the front, back, and sides. These are the muscles responsible for powering all twisting and bending movements, as well as for maintaining stillness when necessary.

Gluteus Maximus (Glutes): These are the powerful muscles of the backside. When you run, your foot hits the ground and anchors there, just for a moment. As this occurs, your gluteus maximus contracts, which shoves your hips—and the rest of your body—forward and past your planted foot. The gluteus maximus can generate tremendous power to propel you forward, but if this muscle is not doing its job correctly, then the other muscles farther down the chain may become strained and injured as they try to compensate.

Lower Back or Lumbar Region (Erector Spinae): These are the muscles of the lower back. They are responsible for straightening you up when you are bent over. They are a powerful muscle group but are particularly vulnerable to injury, especially if they have been injured in the past.

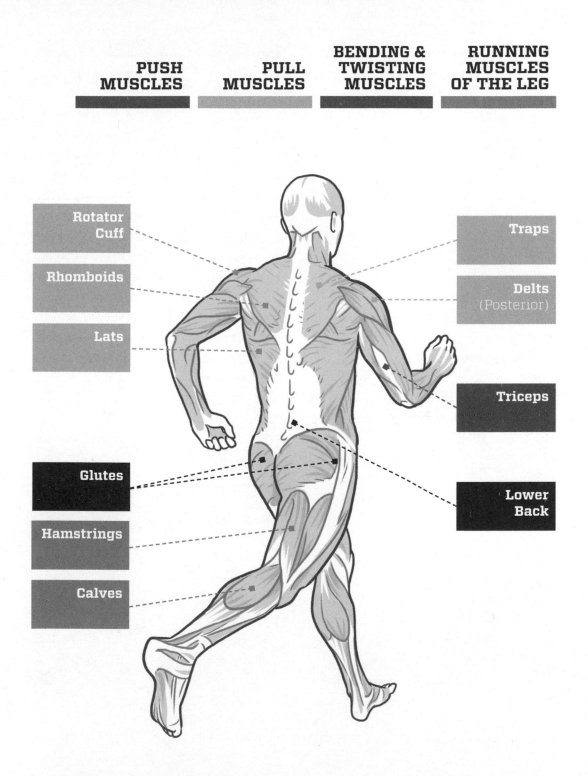

PUSH MUSCLES

PULL MUSCLES

BENDING & TWISTING MUSCLES

RUNNING MUSCLES OF THE LEG

Rotator Cuff

Rhomboids

Lats

Glutes

Hamstrings

Calves

Traps

Delts (Posterior)

Triceps

Lower Back

Rectus Abdominus: This muscle, also known as the "six-pack," is located on the front of your midsection, from the base of your ribs down to your groin. This muscle flexes your spine and enables you to curl up in a ball. People often associate a well-defined rectus abdominus with good health and strength, so this is the muscle many people crave to have toned when beach weather comes around.

Obliques: These muscles, also known as "love handles," are found on the sides of the body above the hips. They are responsible for bending your torso laterally from one side to the other.

Transverse Abdominus: These are the deepest layer of abdominal muscles in the body. They run laterally around the midsection like a girdle. They are primarily engaged when you are trying to balance: They hold your body still against any force that is pulling it off-line.

To feel them, stand up and assume a relaxed position. Let your belly hang out, and breathe easily. Lightly place your hand on your belly, barely touching it. Now, slowly pull your stomach inward just enough to pull it away from your hand. Keep that position, and let your hand drop to your side.

Do you still feel tightness in your abdominals? That's your transverse abdominus working. If you aim to engage these muscles when you are running—and you should in order to ensure that your pelvis is in the right position—then aim to replicate this feeling.

Engaging the transverse abdominus might not be easy at first; it requires some concentration and focus. Aim to maintain engagement for 30 seconds to 1 minute at a time at first, and then slowly increase that time. Soon this movement will feel natural. A good place to practice this is during periods of your strength training workout or during your easy training runs.

Hip Flexors (Iliopsoas, Rectus Femoris, Sartorias, and Tensor Fasciae Latae): These are the muscles found primarily in front of the hip, connecting the femur bone of the upper leg to the spine. They are part of a group that together pulls your knee upward, which makes them crucial to the running motion.

The Running Muscles of the Legs

By now you know that the body does not "think" of itself as a collection of distinct muscles working independently. Instead, the body recruits various muscle groups to perform different functions together.

Therefore, it is somewhat artificial to discuss your leg muscles separately, in isolation from the movements that they perform together. That is why I have framed the following discussion of the leg muscles around the running movements that use them. Although you have been aware of your legs and what they do since you were a toddler, there are other muscles farther up the chain that help move your leg, such as the hip flexors and extensors. Keep this in mind as we discuss the muscles found farther down the chain. It will help you understand the value of doing complex movements because working one body part can affect other related groups as well.

Forward Leg Swing: This involves flexing (bending) your hip and extending (straightening) your knee as your leg comes forward and straightens out as it prepares for touchdown.

Hip flexion was discussed earlier. Knee extension involves four major muscles found on the front of your leg that together are known as the **quadriceps (quads)**. In addition to extending your knee, the quads also stabilize your knee, especially on impact. This is why downhill running can leave the front of your legs sore for several days.

Leg Extension and Push-Off: This involves extending (straightening) your hip and flexing (bending) your knee as your body grabs the ground and pushes off. Hip extension was discussed earlier with the glutes. Knee flexion occurs as the follow-through of push-off and involves three major muscle groups on the back of

the upper leg that together are known as the **hamstrings**.

Foot Push-Off and Recovery: Along with the quads, the muscles of your lower leg help absorb the impact of landing during running and help stabilize your foot and ankle on touchdown. Once your foot touches the ground while running, your body passes over it as momentum carries your body forward. Your heel begins to lift, and you are left standing on your toes in a motion called "plantar flexion."

Your ankle joint is a class-one lever, with the fulcrum of your joint located between the force (the muscles of your calf) and the object to be moved (the push-off occurring at your forefoot and toes). This kind of lever delivers great leverage, which you demonstrate every time you lift your entire body with your calf muscles by standing on your toes.

While you are running, the muscles of your **calf**—the outer calf (gastrocnemius) and the inner calf (soleus)—help lift your heel and push down against your toes to generate propulsion.

Once the push-off phase is completed and your leg swings forward, your foot flexes upward to the toes-up position in the motion called "dorsiflexion" to prepare your foot for landing once again. The muscle that is primarily responsible for this movement of your ankle and foot is the **tibialis anterior**, located on the shin.

These are not the only muscles involved in running, but they are the main ones to know about. Let's put everything together now by revisiting the running motion we reviewed earlier, but with identification of the muscles involved in each phase.

- **The swing phase.** Your toe leaves the ground, and your leg swings forward. Hip flexion occurs first, involving contraction of the iliopsoas, followed by knee extension, powered by the quads, and toe-raising (ankle dorsiflexion), involving contraction of the shin muscle (tibialis anterior).

- **The foot contact phase.** Your heel makes contact with the ground, and your body's full weight is rested on that foot. Your quads and calf muscles are recruited to absorb impact. Your gluteus medius is engaged to stabilize your body laterally.

- **The midfoot loading phase.** Your body moves from placing full weight on your foot through the beginning of push-off. Plantar flexion of the ankle is initiated by the calf muscles, and hip extension is powered by the gluteus maximus.

- **The toe-off phase.** Your heel leaves the ground, and your toes push off as your body moves forward. This involves extension of your hip as the gluteus maximus contracts and flexion of your knee by the hamstrings.

- **Other muscle recruitment.** During all these phases, your abdominal muscles—particularly the transverse abdominus—and **adductors** (inner thigh) are engaged in holding your trunk and hips steady and stable. Also, your shoulders rotate as your arms swing to provide counterbalance to your legs, and your biceps remain contracted to flex your elbows, effectively shortening the length of your arms and reducing the amount of the energy that is required to swing them while running.

Understanding the phases of the running movement and being able to identify which muscles are engaged in each phase will give you an appreciation for the exercises that you need to do to strengthen these muscle groups. You will also have an easier time identifying which muscles are bothering you when an ache or pain flares up.

Exercises that target each of these specific phases not only strengthen the muscles that are directly engaged; they also imprint correct form on the neurons involved in the movement. For this reason, they are not just exercises—they are also good practice for running.

We have shifted from a discussion of **anatomy,** which involves identifying and

No, it isn't. Although many forms of yoga build great core strength and improve balance and functional strength, as well as increase flexibility, yoga is not an adequate substitute for a complete, targeted strength training program.

There are many different modes of strength training. Using your own body as resistance, as yoga does, is a great way to build strength that is appropriate for runners, but it is only one of the available modes. As much as I appreciate yoga and all that it can accomplish—and there are exercises in our program that echo or borrow from yoga—there are things that yoga does not do. For example, yoga does not mimic specific phases of the running motion to improve form and applied strength, and it does not target in an active manner all the muscle groups we have discussed.

If you are currently doing yoga, there is no need to stop—there are certainly benefits to be gained. But read through this book and circle the exercises that you are currently *not* doing in any way, shape, or form through yoga, and add all of those to your routine.

---

locating muscles, to **kinesiology,** which is the study of bodies in motion. This is the difference between appreciating a beautiful sports car in the showroom and taking it on the road for a drive.

Even though there may be some overlap among all these groups, each of the training approaches explained here involves a different fitness target, and each will contribute in different ways to the overall goal of improved running form and speed.

In the workouts that follow, you will see a mix of exercises from each of these groups. The workouts are designed to improve strength and fitness in a variety of ways, and just as a nutritious meal includes a variety of foods, the mix of exercises here will make your workouts not only more effective but also more interesting.

Let's take a breather—you have covered a lot of territory. The next chapter will get you into the nuts and bolts of what the program entails and how to get started.

Before anything else,
preparation is the key to success.

ALEXANDER GRAHAM BELL

GETTING
STARTED

2

Now that we have a better idea about what strength training is and why runners benefit from it, let's review the equipment that you will need for your workouts and how this book will help you use it to get the job done.

The Tools

All the items listed here can be purchased at a sporting goods store; many can be bought used or at a significant discount online. In some cases, it is possible to rig up homemade versions of these tools. However you acquire them, your total investment in this equipment should be no more than the money you spend on entry into a year's worth of races or the cost of a few pairs of shoes. That is a small price to pay for the benefits that you will enjoy from using this equipment and is probably far less than you might have to pay if you end up having to go to a doctor instead to treat a running injury.

BOSU and Wobble Board

These provide an unstable platform to stand on, which forces the muscles of your core and legs to get engaged. Just about any exercise that you can do standing on the ground you can also do standing on a BOSU or on a wobble board.

The BOSU has an inflated dome. Its name is an acronym, shorthand for Both Sides Up, meaning the BOSU can be used either with the flat side down or the inflated side down.

Standing on the soft side is difficult, as each foot and leg has to work independently to help the exerciser maintain balance, but many people find that standing on the platform side, with the soft side on the ground, is even more challenging. In this position the amount of surface area in contact with the ground is greatly reduced, making the exerciser work even harder for balance.

Do not be afraid to flip the BOSU. Doing so will make you a stronger runner in the end. And with practice, you will get better at it.

The wobble board is a solid disc on top of an inverted half sphere. It is a simple piece of equipment yet very challenging to master. Simply standing on the wobble board while not allowing its edges to touch the ground is difficult.

Wobble boards are available in various diameters, ranging from 15 inches to 20 inches. The larger the board, the larger the surface area is relative to the size of the half dome underneath and the distance off the ground. That means the smaller the board, the more difficult it is to balance on it. Some retailers sell wobble board sets, which include a range of board sizes to accommodate a variety of fitness levels and exercises.

Stability Ball

Also known as a Swiss Ball, this piece of equipment provides an unstable alternative to benches and seats. As we discussed, lying on a standard weight bench relieves the abdominals and legs of the need to stay engaged. The stability ball addresses that. Basically, just about anything you can do

If you are a do-it-yourself kind of person, constructing a wobble board should be a piece of cake. Here is one way to do it:

- Using half-inch-thick plywood, cut a circle with a 16-inch diameter (a square with the same width would work also, although it would be a little more limited in its use because it would be more stable than a disc when either side touched down).

- Cut a series of four circles out of a similar piece of plywood, in the following sizes: 5 inches, 4 inches, 3 inches, and 2 inches. Use wood glue to bond these together in descending order, with each circle centered on the next larger one. Drive a 2-inch wood screw through the

center of the discs, making sure to countersink the screw so that its head is below the surface.

- Finally, glue the half dome you have constructed onto the center of your large, 16-inch disc, with the largest-diameter side of the half dome against the disc. Then flip your new wobble board over and drive two screws through from the top through the platform and into the half dome. Be sure to place these screws at least a half inch to either side of the center so as not to contact the other screw you have placed.

sitting or lying down on a bench you can do on a stability ball.

The stability ball can also be used to target specific muscle groups. You can put your feet or hands on the ball in different ways to target your hip flexors, lower back, or upper body. This is one of the most versatile training tools you will own.

Medicine Ball

This small, weighted ball covered in tough rubber is available in a variety of weights, from as little as 5 or 6 pounds to as much as 20 pounds or more. It ranges in size as well, although it is generally just a bit smaller than a basketball.

A medicine ball can be used as a platform in certain exercises and as weighted resistance in others. In this sense, it is more useful than dumbbells because you can use a medicine ball to do most of the dumbbell exercises we will discuss, whereas you cannot use a dumbbell to do all the medicine ball exercises we are going to do. If your available storage space and budget require that you make a choice between a medicine ball and a set of dumbbells, choose the medicine ball.

Dumbbells

As mentioned, having a set of dumbbells is not absolutely necessary to successfully complete this program. However, if you decide to buy them, consider getting adjustable dumbbells or buying sev-

eral different sizes. As you will see, the resistance level that one muscle will find challenging might be a piece of cake for another muscle group.

Exercise Mat

Once you have everything you need for your workout, think about the surface that you will be exercising on.

I recommend that you invest in a thick foam exercise mat—the thicker and firmer, the better. Although a yoga mat would be better than a hard floor, you will not regret investing in a heavier mat. Your knees, elbows, and tailbone will thank you.

Is That Really Everything I Need?

Yes, it is. But that does not mean that there aren't other products and pieces of equipment that could also work well for you. All it takes is a quick trip to a sporting goods store to see that there are many more options available than are on our short list. There are other balancing products, elastic bands, abdominal rolling

If it is within your means, the easiest thing to do may be to order the necessary items online and have them shipped to your door. If this is not an option, there are several good alternatives available to you.

First, look for these items in discount stores. Exercise equipment has moved beyond only sporting goods stores and is now offered by many other retailers, often at deep discounts. Look around.

Second, buy these items used. Because there is nothing electronic or complicated about the equipment we will be using, what you see is likely what you will get. Check out online classified pages, flea markets, and yard sales, or post a want ad of your own. Many people buy exercise equipment impulsively and soon are eager to unload it to a home where it will get more use. Like yours.

wheels, and strap systems, among other offerings. I have used many of these and liked them. But they are not essential for our purposes here.

If you are feeling adventurous and want to try some of these other training options, go ahead. But here is a word of caution: Make sure that you fully understand how the equipment is supposed to be used and that you are careful to do the movements properly. The downside of doing exercises that destabilize your body and work your core is that if you do the movement incorrectly, you can injure yourself. Also, be sure to continue doing the exercises discussed in this book instead of substituting new exercises. This will ensure that you strengthen your body for healthy running.

Finding Time and Space

Having the best equipment in the world will not be of much use if you do not have a place where you can use it. In a perfect world, you would have a separate space set aside exclusively for your workouts, bathed in natural light, with a rubberized floor, big windows with southern exposure, floor-to-ceiling mirrors, custom ventilation, and a watercooler. But for most of us, that is not the case.

When it comes to space, the equipment required for these workouts will not take up a lot of room; most of it can be easily stored in a closet or under a bed. (In the case of the stability ball, it might even double as usable furniture.) Also, the workouts themselves do not require a lot of elbow room; a dozen square feet will do the trick, which might only require that you move a coffee table or chair.

The workouts are also fairly quiet, so if you share space with other people—roommates or family—you can keep from disturbing them. They might even become curious about what you are doing. If you invite them to work out with you, you can help them establish healthy habits themselves as well as create shared time that makes the workouts more than just about fitness.

Timing is trickier. Planning a whole day around every workout is not very realistic. More often, we struggle to find a few free moments to ourselves to work out, and even then we have to share space with our furniture and our families, which often leaves us bumping up against both. At these times, you might find it difficult to do even part of your workout.

Do not let that stop you. Even a short workout is much better than no workout at all, so do not aim for perfection in each session. The workouts here are designed to take a little more than 1 minute per set to complete, and the minimum for a productive workout is about 12 sets, so if you can get in a quick 15 minutes, you will be on target. If you can do more than the minimum—or even the full workout specified for each day—all the better.

This program is based on scheduling 2 workouts per week, for a total of 16 workouts during the length of the 8-week program. Schedule these workouts at least 1 day apart in order to give your body sufficient time to rest and recover between these efforts. If you have the time and motivation to add a third day of training, you may do so by repeating the first workout of the week, as long as you schedule all the workouts at least 1 full day apart from each other.

Even though it is okay to schedule these workouts on your off days from running, I recommend that you take at least 1 day a week off completely from all training. The concept of "active rest," in which you substitute one form of training for another in order to give some muscles a break, is really an oxymoron. Because, as we have seen, the body likes to recruit many different muscles to perform its movements, only true downtime from all exercise really provides the body with a chance to heal and recharge itself.

On the other hand, if you have a difficult training day planned, it might be advisable to stack the strength training on top of it. This will make the day marginally harder but will also open up the possibility of taking the following day off entirely, or at least free from hard training. This is why many people choose to do strength training on days when they have scheduled their speed work, tempo runs, or long runs.

The question often comes up about what time of day is best to do these workouts. The quick answer is any time you can squeeze them in. But I recommend morning, when you first wake up. You can multitask by listening to the news while you are working out; a single news cycle is more than enough time to get this done, and by doing your workout first thing in the morning, you avoid a common pitfall: having unexpected obstacles develop during the day that sidetrack your plans. You know what I mean: A project is thrown on your lap at work, social plans suddenly arise, or a crisis at home requires your attention.

Also, food might become an issue. By the time you get home at night, it has probably been hours since you last ate. You want to work out, but you are starving. And if you eat, then you will not feel comfortable working out. You can eat and wait, but then you will be working out right before bedtime, which might leave you wide awake when you should be sleeping. In the end you decide to skip the workout and try to get back on schedule the next day. Working out in the morning avoids all these problems. If you are a bit hungry, have something light, such as a small glass of juice, a cup of yogurt, or a slice of bread, and then you will be good to go.

Finally, on days when you are also running, should you do this workout before or after your run? The answer is that it really depends on your own preferences. Some people like to use the strength workout as a warm-up before a run, but if getting out of bed to meet your running group is hard enough in the morning, then getting up 20 minutes earlier probably will not sound very appealing. Others like to ease into their morning run and finish with strength training. A third option is to keep these workouts completely separate and do them at different times of the day. Experiment with different formulas, and see what works best for you.

The Next 8 Weeks—and Beyond

Now that you understand the value of strength training to runners, how the body moves to accomplish work and especially to run, and what you need in order to get started, it is time to introduce the nuts and bolts of our program: the exercises and the routines that you will be doing.

These exercises are challenging. If you have had any injury to your lower back, heart problems, or any other medical condition that may affect your ability to safely perform these exercises, please consult your physician before undertaking this program.

Chapter 3 introduces the exercises. Flip through this chapter several times to become familiar with the exercises and their variants. Then set aside some time to practice the basic form of each exercise—not as a workout but as a way of familiarizing yourself with the movements and becoming accustomed to how they feel when done properly. As the saying goes, only perfect practice makes perfect, so do not rush right into the workouts; they will come soon enough.

Once you have got the basics down, you can begin incorporating strength training into your routine. As you will see in Chapter 4, the workouts in this book are organized in a progressive format, based on an 8-week training cycle. Much like endurance training, the schedule here is structured on progressively harder workouts that peak near the end of the program.

The exercises in the workouts roll out with an assumption that you may not have any past experience with these movements. If this is not the case for you—if you have done these before and have established competency with the basic movements and you find that they are not challenging enough for you—do not step back from your current level of fitness in order to begin at the start of the program. Instead, pick a more advanced form of the exercise. Avoid being too ambitious, however; this is an 8-week program, and I want you to be as enthusiastic by the end as you are in the beginning. Do not set yourself up for burnout by jumping too far ahead.

If you are in your off-season or maintenance phase of your training, without a race coming up on your calendar, this is the perfect time for you to get familiar with strength training. Without having to acclimate to increasingly difficult running loads, your body is ready to take on the challenge of progressively harder strength workouts in a format called **periodization**. Following this format, you enter into training cycles—8 weeks long, in the program presented here—using progressively more challenging versions of each exercise on each cycle. At the end of the 8-week cycle, you could take an easy week of lighter training; then begin the next cycle at a more intense level.

By alternating stress loads in this manner, you save wear and tear on your body and keep from exhausting it beyond its ability to adapt and improve. But the effect is not just physical: By scheduling changes in your routine and by taking breaks from more intense training, you can improve your fitness without getting bored or burned out.

If you decide to register for a race, continue incorporating strength training into your routine as part of your race preparation. Some coaches might advise you to use strength training only during the early part of training and then to drop off from strength training as you enter your race season, but I disagree with that approach. As the saying goes, dance with the date that brought you. If strength training kept you strong and healthy, it does not make sense to abandon it; that would only open the door to losing strength and leaving yourself vulnerable once more to injury.

To work this 8-week program into your race preparation, just scroll back 9 weeks from the date of your target race. That is the date for your first strength workout for that cycle.

When you reach the end of the program 8 weeks later, you will be 1 week away from your race. At this point you should be in your taper period, when you would be cutting back on your volume. Even if your taper began 1 or 2 weeks earlier, it is appropriate to continue strength training until 1 week from race day because these workouts keep you physically and mentally sharp without causing enough muscle fatigue to slow you down on race day.

Ultimately, the best program is the one that best fits your lifestyle and preferences and that delivers the best results. The options available when deciding on how to structure a workout are nearly endless. This book takes the guesswork and anxiety out of putting together a strength training routine by presenting a detailed, focused plan to get you on track.

But that is not the only way to use this book. If you would prefer to design your own workout routine, this book presents enough information to enable you to do that. Once you are comfortable with all the exercises and their more advanced variants, you can put together your own effective, purposeful, and structured strength training program. Just be sure to include exercises that target all the major muscle groups that we discuss here.

However you choose to use this book, be sure to maintain proper form in every motion you make. In the following pages you will read not only about how to do each exercise, but also about how *not* to do it. Please give both of these discussions equal attention.

In the end, I hope that you come to enjoy the challenge of strength training as much as I have and that you will decide to make it part of your long-term fitness lifestyle.

As long as I run,
I will always lift weights.

FLORENCE GRIFFITH JOYNER
Olympian and world record holder in the
100 meter and 200 meter sprints

THE 3
EXERCISES

This chapter will present and explain the exercises that make up the workout routines in Chapter 4. Together the two chapters will help you develop the comprehensive strength you need to get faster and to run without injury.

Each exercise will be presented in its basic form, with an explanation of how it is to be performed and what pitfalls to avoid. Also included with each exercise will be tips to help you master the forms, as well as advanced variants, which are to be attempted only when you have mastered the basic forms.

Remember, there is no need to rush this process. As long as you are challenging yourself, at whatever level, you are improving.

STANDING AND WEIGHTED
EXERCISES

TORSO TWISTS

MUSCLE TARGETS: Abs (transverse), delts, biceps, triceps
EQUIPMENT: Medicine ball or dumbbell, BOSU (advanced)

 # REPS 14–20

FORM

1

Hold a medicine ball or dumbbell in front of you with both hands, keeping your arms parallel to the ground.

2

Swing the weight smoothly and forcefully from right to left and back again.

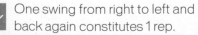

One swing from right to left and back again constitutes 1 rep.

ADVANCED FORM

■ Perform the exercise while standing on either side of a BOSU.

Tip

Your muscles are most engaged when you stop sharply, so as you swing, imagine that you are standing against a wall that you will hit with the dumbbell if you do not stop yourself.

WEIGHTED SWINGS

MUSCLE TARGETS: Obliques, abs (transverse), delts, biceps, triceps

EQUIPMENT: Medicine ball or dumbbell, BOSU (advanced)

FORM

1

Stand with your feet 2"–3" apart and your knees slightly bent, holding a dumbbell or medicine ball with both hands near your outer hip.

2

Now swing the weight up diagonally toward the opposite side. Just as with any sport that requires swinging with both arms together, such as baseball and golf, aim to keep your arms as straight as possible through the swing, especially during the middle phase of the movement, when your arms are in front of you.

Return to the start position. Complete all swings on one side, then repeat on the other side.

ADVANCED FORM

- Perform this movement while standing on either side of a BOSU.

Tip

Keep your eyes on the weight as you swing, and aim to swing your body as a single unit. Do not just swing your arms; think of them as welded into place with your shoulders.

DEADLIFTS AND FRONT RAISES

MUSCLE TARGETS: Lower back, hamstrings, traps, delts, biceps, triceps

EQUIPMENT: Dumbbell or medicine ball, BOSU (advanced)

FORM

1

Stand with your feet a bit wider than shoulder-width. Tilt your pelvis backward and arch your back, with your knees slightly bent. Keep your pelvis tilted throughout the exercise, even as you straighten up and bend over again.

2

Bend forward at the hips, being careful not to round your back. Grip a dumbbell or medicine ball with both hands.

3

Straighten and raise the weight up over your head toward the ceiling in one smooth movement. When the weight is at the highest point of the movement, your back should still be slightly arched and your pelvis tilted backward.

Hold for a moment, then let the weight swing back down. This constitutes 1 rep.

ADVANCED FORM

■ Perform this movement from atop a BOSU, either side up.

Tip

To get accustomed to the deadlift position, practice gripping your sides with your thumbs at the back of your obliques and bend over.

COACH'S NOTE

This exercise combines two exercises into one complex movement. Our program does not incorporate the Deadlift as a stand-alone exercise because the major muscles used to perform the Deadlift—the glutes and the lower back muscles—can generate so much power that you need a heavy weight to challenge them; that kind of weight is usually found only in a gym. Instead, we get results by making the exercise more complex.

ONE-LEGGED DEADLIFTS

MUSCLE TARGETS: Lower back, glutes (medius)

EQUIPMENT: None

FORM

1

Stand on your left leg, with your knee slightly bent so that your leg muscles are engaged to hold your body steady.

2

Keeping your right leg straight and your arms at your sides, bend over, raising your right leg behind you as you lower your upper body, forming a T. Keep your back straight throughout the movement.

 Rise back up. This constitutes 1 rep. When you have reached your goal number of reps, repeat on your right leg.

ADVANCED FORMS

■ Perform this exercise without touching down with the other leg when you return to the starting position. This forces you to engage your stabilizing muscles even more as you work on maintaining balance throughout the exercise.

■ Perform this exercise with your arms straight out at your sides, and when you are bent over, rotate your upper body so that you first point downward with one arm, then downward with the other. This shifts your center of gravity from one side to the other during the exercise, which makes your core work harder.

Tip

However much you think you are raising your leg behind you, it probably needs to be raised higher.

COACH'S NOTE

This exercise is also known as the Tipping Bird, after the children's toy of the same name. You can also imagine yourself as a seesaw.

THE PHOENIX

MUSCLE TARGETS: Hamstrings, glutes, quads, delts (medial)

EQUIPMENT: Dumbbells (light), BOSU (advanced)

 # REPS 10-20

FORM

1
Perform a squat, holding two light dumbbells at your sides.

2
As you rise, lift the weights up and outward, raising them to eye level by the time you are standing up fully. This movement of the dumbbells, without the squat, is known as a **Lateral Raise.**

Lower the weights to your sides as you squat, returning to starting position. This constitutes 1 rep.

ADVANCED FORMS

- Perform this exercise from atop one side of a BOSU.

- Work an additional part of the delts (anterior) by raising the dumbbells in front of you in a movement called a **Front Raise**. It can be alternated here with the lateral raise movement. Front Raises also destabilize you in a way that Lateral Raises do not because Front Raises shift your center of gravity forward, putting more pressure on your lower back.

Tip

Maintain proper form during the Squat: Stand with your feet shoulder-width apart, your back arched and pelvis tilted backward. Bend your knees and sink downward. Focus your eyes straight ahead or upward. Do not sink lower than when your knees get to a 90-degree angle; going lower puts excess strain on your knees, with no extra gain in strength.

SQUATS AND SHOULDER PRESSES

REPS
10-20

MUSCLE TARGETS: Hamstrings, glutes, quads, delts, triceps

EQUIPMENT: Dumbbells, BOSU (advanced)

FORM

1

Hold the weights by your shoulders and squat. Remember to keep your back arched, your pelvis tilted backward, and your eyes focused straight ahead or upward. Do not let your knees bend lower than a 90-degree angle.

2

As you rise, push the weights upward toward the ceiling, bringing them together overhead in an arcing motion.

Lower the weights to your shoulders as you squat down to complete the rep.

ADVANCED FORMS

■ Alternate sets with a dumbbell in one hand only. This destabilizes your body laterally, forcing your core to work harder to keep you from falling over sideways.

■ Perform this exercise from atop either side of a BOSU.

Tip

Follow the weights with your eyes as you press them upward. This helps you push them straight up, rather than letting them drift forward. This alignment helps keep your delts fully engaged without putting too much strain on your triceps.

COACH'S NOTE

Like The Phoenix, this exercise combines two separate movements into one complex exercise, but this is a more complex movement than The Phoenix because it involves flexion and extension of an additional joint: the elbow. Because more muscle mass is engaged here than in The Phoenix, you can use heavier weights here than you would use in that other exercise.

THE DISCUS-THROWER

> **MUSCLE TARGETS:** Glutes, quads, obliques, abs (transverse), delts (medial, posterior)
> **EQUIPMENT:** Dumbbell

**# REPS
10-20**

FORM

1

Scissor your legs so that one foot is in front of you—spread your legs and give yourself plenty of room.

2

Hold a dumbbell in the arm opposite your outstretched leg and squat, twisting your body so that you are holding the dumbbell on the outside of the opposite knee, with your palm facing inward toward that knee.

3

Stand up while twisting your body and raising the dumbbell. Lead with the elbow of the arm holding the dumbbell, rotating your arm so that your hand is the highest part of your body.

Return to the starting position. This constitutes 1 rep. Complete your goal number of reps, then switch the dumbbell to your other hand.

ADVANCED FORM

■ Perform this exercise with your eyes closed. This is difficult and disorienting, but the effect is to make you more aware of your body position.

COACH'S NOTE

This exercise gets its name from the similarity that the starting position of this exercise has to the classic form of a discus-thrower, although the weight is in the opposite hand.

ARM CIRCLES/REVERSE ARM CIRCLES

MUSCLE TARGETS: Delts (anterior), abs (transverse)

EQUIPMENT: Dumbbell or medicine ball, BOSU (advanced)

FORM

1
Hold a dumbbell or medicine ball with both hands, and stand with your feet shoulder-width apart.

2
Extend your elbows to straighten your arms, then draw a large clockwise circle with the weight.

One revolution constitutes 1 rep. For **Reverse Arm Circles**, do the same basic movement, but draw counterclockwise circles.

ADVANCED FORMS

■ Perform this exercise while standing with your feet close together. Doing so reduces the size of your foundation, making you less stable and making your core work harder.

■ Perform this exercise while standing on either side of a BOSU. Again, the closer your feet are, the harder—and more effective—this exercise is.

Tip

The larger the radius of the circle you draw, the greater the impact on your abdominal muscles.

WALKING LUNGES

MUSCLE TARGETS: Glutes, quads, hamstrings, lower back, abs (transverse)
EQUIPMENT: Medicine ball (advanced)

**# SETS
1-2**

FORM

 1
Locate a stretch of floor that is at least 30 feet long. Keep your eyes focused on a distant point that is at eye level, and hold your arms either straight out in front of your body or raised out to your sides.

2
Take a long step forward, being sure not to let your front knee go past your toes on that leg.

↻ Walk to your goal turnaround point and return. This constitutes 1 set.

ADVANCED FORM

■ Stretch out your arms in front of you while holding a medicine ball. Step forward with your right leg, and after you have descended, swing your arms and upper body toward your right, over the extended leg. You should be facing to the right, with your upper body and arms perpendicular to the line you are walking. Swing back to the front and step forward with your left leg; then swing toward your left in the same way.

Tip

Concentrate on bending your back knee and sinking straight downward instead of bending forward over your front knee. This helps keep your front knee from passing forward of your front foot and reduces strain on your knee.

COACH'S NOTE

This exercise is similar to the Squat we did in the Squats and Shoulder Presses exercise, but it introduces more movement and so is less stable.

SIDE LUNGES

MUSCLE TARGETS: Quads, glutes, adductors

EQUIPMENT: Medicine ball or dumbbell (advanced)

**# REPS
10–20**

FORM

1

Stand with your feet close together, your knees slightly bent and your back slightly arched.

2

Step out to the left, keeping your right leg straight as you bend your left knee down to a 90-degree angle.

3

Step back up to your starting position and lunge out to the right, keeping your left leg straight this time as you bend your right knee.

Return to the standing position. This constitutes 1 rep.

ADVANCED FORM

■ Hold a medicine ball or dumbbell close to your chest as you perform this movement in order to increase the resistance and the challenge to your core and legs.

Tip

Keep your feet facing forward as you step out to one side, then the other. This will put more stress on the outer hip, where we want it.

COACH'S NOTE

This exercise is similar to the standard Squat but focuses more directly on the lateral stabilizers, especially the gluteus medius.

LATERAL LEG SWINGS

MUSCLE TARGET: Glutes (medius)
EQUIPMENT: BOSU (advanced)

**# REPS
20-30**

FORM

1

Standing on your left leg, swing your right leg across your midline.

2

Swing your right leg outward as far as possible, and then swing it back across your midline toward your left side, returning to the starting position.

This constitutes 1 rep. Complete your target number of reps, then switch to the other leg.

ADVANCED FORM

■ Stand on either side of a BOSU while performing this exercise.

Tip

Maintaining balance is a challenge with this exercise. Not only are you standing on one leg, but also the movement of your other leg shifts your center of gravity. Try picking a spot on the floor about 6 feet or so in front of you to focus on during the exercise. This will help you maintain your balance.

COACH'S NOTE

This exercise is designed to improve your balance and the range of motion in your hips, as well as increase the strength in your gluteus medius. Think of your leg as a pendulum, and let the momentum of your movement bring your leg as far as possible.

FRONT LEG SWINGS

MUSCLE TARGETS: Hip flexors, glutes

EQUIPMENT: BOSU (advanced)

FORM

1
Standing on your left leg, swing your right leg behind you, then swing it forward as far as you comfortably can. Return to the starting position.

This constitutes 1 rep. Complete your target number of reps, then switch to the other leg.

ADVANCED FORM

- Stand on either side of a BOSU while performing this exercise.

Tip

If you find it difficult to maintain balance, try counterswinging your arms during this movement: As you swing your right leg forward, swing your left arm forward along with it. Think of your leg as a pendulum, and aim to use momentum to gain as wide a range of motion as possible.

COACH'S NOTE

Like the Lateral Leg Swing, this exercise helps improve hip flexibility and strength along with balance.

STANDING HURDLES

↘ **MUSCLE TARGETS:** Glutes, hip flexors
EQUIPMENT: BOSU (advanced)

 # REPS 20-30

FORM

1

Stand on your left leg and bring your right knee up and out to your right.

2

Keeping that knee bent, swing it forward, then down and back, drawing a large counterclockwise circle. The motion should be Out, Up, Forward, Down, Back.

↻ Complete all reps on one leg, then repeat on the other leg.

ADVANCED FORM

- Stand on either side of a BOSU while performing this exercise.

COACH'S NOTE

This exercise opens up your hips to increase range of motion and improve flexibility.

STANDING REVERSE HURDLES

MUSCLE TARGETS: Glutes, hip flexors

EQUIPMENT: BOSU (advanced)

 # REPS 20-30

FORM

1
Stand on your left leg and bring your right knee up and forward.

2
Keeping that knee bent, swing it outward, then down and back, drawing a large clockwise circle. The motion should be Up and Forward, Outward, Down.

Complete all reps on one leg, then repeat on the other leg.

ADVANCED FORM

■ Stand on either side of a BOSU while performing this exercise.

Tip

Balance and range of motion are more important than the number of reps you perform, so do not rush your improvement by adding more reps too quickly.

COACH'S NOTE

As with the Standing Hurdles, this exercise opens up your hips to increase range of motion and improve flexibility.

STEP-UPS

REPS
10-20

MUSCLE TARGETS: Glutes, hip flexors, abs (transverse, rectus), obliques, delts (anterior)

EQUIPMENT: Dumbbells (advanced)

FORM

1

Stand with your elbows bent at a 90-degree angle or less, holding your right arm forward and your left arm back.

2

Scissor your legs, bringing your right leg forward while keeping your left leg back. Note that your arms work in opposition to your legs throughout this movement, just as when you run or walk.

3

Step up forcefully, swinging your left arm forward and your right knee upward.

Reverse to return to the starting position. This constitutes 1 rep. Complete all your target reps on one side, then continue on the other side, reversing your leg and arm positions.

ADVANCED FORM

■ Hold a light pair of dumbbells while performing this exercise, but be sure not to compromise your form as you swing them.

Tip

This exercise should be explosive. The force of your leg swing should bring you upward, almost to the point of jumping in the air. If you are swinging your left knee up, you should find yourself on the toes of your right foot. Do not aim for this position by standing on your toes; instead, increase the power of your knee raise until it actually pulls you upward onto your toes.

COACH'S NOTE

This exercise mimics the running movement, though in an exaggerated form, in order to stress the key muscle groups involved and trigger an adaptation response in them.

PULLOVERS

MUSCLE TARGETS: Delts, triceps, seratus anterior

EQUIPMENT: Dumbbell or medicine ball, stability ball (advanced)

FORM

1 Lie on your exercise mat faceup, with your knees bent and your feet flat on the floor.

2 Hold a weight directly above you with both hands.

3 Keeping your elbows locked in a slightly bent position, draw the weight backward until it almost touches the floor, then pull it back until your arms are pointed straight up to the ceiling once again.

 This constitutes 1 rep.

ADVANCED FORMS

■ Lie faceup on a
stability ball while
performing this
exercise.

Tip

Keep your
elbows locked
in a slightly
bent position
throughout the
movement. If
you bend and
extend your
elbow as you
perform the
movement,
you focus the
exercise on
the triceps
rather than
on the other
major muscle
groups that we
are aiming to
improve.

■ Complete all reps while
holding a dumbbell with
only one hand, then switch
to the other hand.

HIGH REVERSE FLYES

 MUSCLE TARGETS: Delts (posterior), rotator cuff
EQUIPMENT: Dumbbells

FORM

1
Hold a pair of
weights by your lap
while standing.

2
Swing your arms
outward and
upward, turning your
hands so that your
palms face away
from you.

↻ Return the weights down to your lap, turning your
palms back toward each other. This constitutes 1 rep.

ADVANCED FORMS

■ Perform this exercise with one arm at a time to create lateral instability and to increase the challenge to your core.

■ Perform half the reps while standing on one leg and the other half while standing on the other leg. This improves your balance.

Tip

Rotation of your arm strengthens the rotator cuff muscles, but be careful not to overload that area, as it is prone to injury. Do not swing the weights rapidly, and do not attempt to lift heavier weights than you can comfortably use for 14 or more reps. Also, take care not to push your range of motion beyond what you can comfortably do. Err on the side of caution here.

LOW REVERSE FLYES

MUSCLE TARGETS: Traps, rhomboids, lats
EQUIPMENT: Dumbbells

REPS
10-20

FORM

1

Holding a pair of dumbbells low in front of you, bend slightly from the waist while keeping your back arched.

2

Bring the dumbbells together so that your palms are facing each other, and bend your elbows.

3

Swing your arms outward, keeping your elbows bent. You should feel a tightening and compression of the midback muscles between your shoulder blades. Do not raise your hands up high; they remain on that same plane, perpendicular to your body, as you sweep them back and then return them in front of you.

Return to the starting position. This constitutes 1 rep.

ADVANCED FORMS

■ Perform this exercise with only one arm at a time. This pulls your body off-line, resulting in a greater challenge to your core as it struggles to maintain balance.

■ Stand on one leg at a time while performing this exercise. Removing one of your supports challenges your core. Aim for an even number of reps, and perform half of them while standing on one leg and the other half while standing on the other leg.

COACH'S NOTE

Although this is a single joint movement, it can have a big impact on your fitness. It primarily works your midback, targeting the muscles that help you maintain proper posture while running.

DUMBBELL CHEST PRESSES

MUSCLE TARGETS: Pecs, delts (anterior), triceps
EQUIPMENT: Dumbbells, stability ball (advanced)

FORM

1
Hold dumbbells overhead, with your elbows slightly bent.

2
Lower the weights, flaring your elbows outward. Bring the weights down until you feel a stretch across your chest; do not push the range of motion beyond this point because you do not want to risk hyperextending your shoulders.

3
Raise the weights back up to the starting point.

 This constitutes 1 rep.

ADVANCED FORMS

- Perform this exercise with one arm at a time. Holding a single dumbbell, perform your target number of reps; then switch to your other hand. This form destabilizes your body and forces your core to work harder.

- Perform this exercise while lying back on a stability ball. This form engages your core more effectively. Remember to position your head and shoulders on the ball while keeping your hips up in the air.

Tip

Aim to keep your forearms perpendicular to the ground during the exercise in order to ensure that the pressure from the weight flows through your arms down toward the bigger muscles of your chest and shoulders, which can handle more resistance than your arms.

FLOOR EXERCISES

HIP RAISES

MUSCLE TARGETS: Glutes, lower back, abs (transverse)

EQUIPMENT: Medicine ball (advanced)

FORM

1

Lie faceup on your exercise mat, with your knees bent, your legs together, and your feet flat on the floor.

2

Raise your hips in the air until you have achieved a straight line from your knees to your upper body.

Lower down to the starting position. This constitutes 1 rep.

ADVANCED FORMS

- Stretch one leg straight out, and hold it just a couple of inches off the floor. Now push off your other foot and raise your hips up in the air. Perform the target number of reps, then repeat on the other side.

Tip

Be sure to keep the raised leg in the same position throughout; only your hips should be rising up.

- This is similar to the one-legged form above, except with one leg planted on a medicine ball instead of on the floor, which engages the hamstrings of your planted leg as they prevent the ball from rolling away.

COACH'S NOTE

This exercise works the muscles on the back of your body, especially the glutes, while also providing a good stretch for the hip flexor muscles on the front of your body.

PUSH-UPS

MUSCLE TARGETS: Pecs, delts (anterior), triceps, abs, glutes

EQUIPMENT: Stability ball (advanced)

 # REPS
10–100

FORM

1 Lie facedown on an exercise mat, with your palms down on the mat slightly wider than your armpits.

2 Raise your body up by extending your elbows.

After reaching full extension, bend your elbows and lower down to an inch or two above the mat. This constitutes 1 full rep.

ADVANCED FORMS

■ Divide your target number of reps by two, and perform half of them with one leg held an inch or two off the floor. Then immediately continue on to the remaining reps with the other leg upraised. This form engages your core more effectively as it struggles to maintain balance and also provides a good workout for your glutes, which will be working to hold the upraised leg off the floor.

■ Keep your feet on a stability ball while performing this exercise. Making the platform for your feet movable introduces instability, which engages your core even more.

Tip

Keep your chin up during the exercise, turn the heels of your palms slightly outward with your fingers pointed slightly inward, and do not lock your elbows at full extension because this takes the pressure off your muscles and puts it on your joints. Do not arch your back or let your hips sag down. Keep your body rigid, which not only protects your lower back, but also effectively works your core muscles.

CRUNCHES

MUSCLE TARGETS: Abs (rectus)
EQUIPMENT: None

**# REPS
20-50**

FORM

1

Lie faceup on your exercise mat, with your knees bent and your heels on the floor. Cross your arms over your chest.

2

Curl your body upward, being sure to keep your lower back on the floor; then return to the starting position.

This constitutes 1 rep.

ADVANCED FORM

■ When performing this exercise, peel your lower back off the floor and sit all the way up to an upright position, then return down to the starting position. This version is also known as **Roll-Ups**. Keep your arms folded across your chest during this exercise; this will reduce your leverage and the momentum you can generate while performing the movement, which increases the workload on your rectus abdominus and hip flexors.

Tip

You can cradle your head lightly with your hands instead of crossing your arms over your chest, but if you do, be sure not to pull on your head, because that could strain your neck.

CROSSOVER CRUNCHES

MUSCLE TARGETS: Abs (rectus), obliques

EQUIPMENT: None

REPS
20-50

FORM

1

Lie faceup on your exercise mat, with your knees bent and your feet flat on the floor. Cross your right ankle over onto your left knee.

2

Keeping your right elbow on the floor and your left hand on the back of your head, bring your left shoulder up and across diagonally toward your right knee. The goal is to touch your left elbow to your right knee, though actual touching is unnecessary; the key is to bring your shoulder up and across diagonally.

Complete your goal number of reps, then continue on the other side.

ADVANCED FORMS

■ Raise your grounded foot off the floor a few inches while performing this exercise. This engages your hip flexors and rectus abdominus to a greater extent as these muscles work to keep both legs up in the air. The essential movement remains the same, although you might find that crossing over is especially difficult.

■ Keep your right leg extended and perform this exercise by raising your left arm and right leg up, aiming to touch your left elbow to your right knee. This engages your hip flexors in addition to the other muscles used in the standard movement.

■ Hold your body in the crunched position for a count of 5 before returning back to the floor.

KNEE CRUNCHES

MUSCLE TARGETS: Abs (rectus), hip flexors, obliques
EQUIPMENT: None

FORM

Sit on your exercise mat. Stretch your legs out in front of you, with your knees fully extended. Keep your arms at your sides, palms facing downward on the floor.

2

Bring your knees toward your chest, then extend your legs again, keeping your feet off the floor.

Return to the starting position. This constitutes 1 rep.

ADVANCED FORMS

- Keep your upper body off the ground while performing this exercise. This causes you to balance on your backside, which engages your lower back and core even more.

Tip

If you are having trouble keeping in place on the floor, wedge your hands under your backside to keep from sliding around. Eventually, you should be able to fold your arms across your chest, using only core strength to hold your body steady.

- Hold your body in the crunched position for a count of 5 before returning back to the floor.

THE RUSSIAN TWIST

MUSCLE TARGETS: Abs (transverse), delts, biceps, triceps
EQUIPMENT: Medicine ball or dumbbell

FORM

1

Sit on an exercise mat with your knees bent and your heels on the ground. Lean back so that your torso is at a 45-degree angle to the floor, keeping your back as straight as possible.

2

Hold a weight out to your side with both hands.

3

Hold your arms away from your body and swing the weight from one side to the other, coming as close to touching the floor on either side of you as possible without actually touching.

 A swing to both left and right constitutes 1 rep.

ADVANCED FORM

- Keep your feet off the floor, balancing on your backside while performing this movement. This forces your transverse abdominus to work harder to maintain balance while engaging your rectus abdominus to hold your legs in the air.

Tip

To really engage your abdominal muscles, aim to stop sharply on each side.

LEG RAISES

MUSCLE TARGETS: Abs (rectus), hip flexors, quads
EQUIPMENT: None

FORM

1

Lie faceup on your exercise mat, with your hands wedged under your backside and your legs extended.

2

Raise your legs off the floor until they are perpendicular to the ground, then slowly lower them again.

 This constitutes 1 rep.

ADVANCED FORMS

- Instead of anchoring your hands under your backside, clasp them behind your head while performing this exercise. This makes your core work harder to hold your body still as your legs swing up and down.

Tip

If needed, reduce resistance by bending your knees, which will increase your leverage in moving your legs. This makes the exercise a bit easier to perform.

- Place your palms down on your mat to provide a solid base. When your legs are at the apex of their upward swing during this exercise, try to lift your hips off the ground. Use your hands to push off. Then drop your hips and lower your legs. This constitutes 1 rep.

SIDE CRUNCHES

MUSCLE TARGET: Obliques

EQUIPMENT: BOSU (advanced)

REPS
20–50

FORM

1

Lie on your left side on your exercise mat, keeping your body as straight as possible.

2

Simultaneously raise your legs and your shoulders, then lower both back down to the mat.

 This constitutes 1 rep. Complete your target number of reps, then repeat on the other side.

ADVANCED FORMS

■ Perform this exercise while lying on a BOSU.

■ Hold your body in the crunched position for a count of 5 before returning back to the floor.

Tip

You may keep your hand on the floor in front of you for balance, but do not push off that hand to do the exercise. Focus on using your oblique muscles to accomplish the movement.

COACH'S NOTE

If you keep your hands on your side during this exercise, you will feel your obliques contracting. This will confirm that you are working the targeted muscles, and will also help you improve your body awareness.

SIDE LEG RAISES

MUSCLE TARGET: Glutes (medius)

EQUIPMENT: None

 # REPS 10-30

FORM

1

Lie on your side with your legs outstretched, your knees extended, with one leg resting on top of the other.

2

Raise the top leg as high as you comfortably can, then lower it back down again. This constitutes 1 rep.

Complete your target number of reps, then continue on the other side.

ADVANCED FORM

■ Assume a side plank position, resting on your elbow as you hold your body rigid in the air. Perform the movement from this position.

SIDE HIP RAISES

REPS
10-30

MUSCLE TARGETS: Obliques, abs (transverse), glutes (medius)

EQUIPMENT: BOSU (advanced)

FORM

1

Lie on your right side on your exercise mat.

2

Raise your hips in the air to a side plank position, holding your body in a rigid line while resting on your elbow.

3

Lower your hips down to an inch or two off the mat, then raise them back up again. This constitutes 1 rep.

Perform all the target reps on one side, then continue on the other side.

ADVANCED FORMS

■ Have your feet on a BOSU while performing this movement. Doing so destabilizes your base, forcing your body to recruit your core to a greater degree to maintain balance.

Tip

Make sure that your elbow is directly below your shoulder. If it is even slightly higher, you have a much harder time holding your form. Also, that position places too much stress on your shoulder.

■ Hold your opposite arm in the air while performing this movement. By putting a percentage of your body weight farther from your center, you decrease your leverage over your body and raise the challenge for your core in its effort to hold your body stable in space.

ADDUCTOR LEG RAISES

MUSCLE TARGET: Adductors

EQUIPMENT: None

FORM

1

Lie on your left side. Bend your right knee and point it at the ceiling while placing your right foot on the floor in front of your left knee. This gets your right leg out of the way so that your left leg can do the target exercise.

2

Keep your left knee extended and raise your left leg up as high as possible, and then lower it again. This constitutes 1 rep.

 Complete the target number of reps, then repeat on the other side.

ADVANCED FORM

- Hold your leg in the upright position for 5–10 seconds during each rep.

Tip

Keep the foot of your moving leg rotated, with your heel pointed upward.

COACH'S NOTE

Most people find that they are relatively stronger on adductor (squeezing) leg movements than abductor (spreading) leg movements. Take this into account when performing adductor and abductor exercises; plan to perform up to 50 percent more repetitions in the adductor leg raise set than you performed on the side leg (abductor) set.

LEG CIRCLES

MUSCLE TARGETS: Abs (transverse, rectus), hip flexors, quads

EQUIPMENT: None

FORM

1

Lie faceup on your exercise mat, with your arms outstretched and your palms down on the mat. Keep your knees extended and your legs together and as straight as possible.

2

Raise your legs slightly off the floor, and draw a big clockwise or counterclockwise circle in the air with your feet.

 One full circle constitutes 1 rep.

ADVANCED FORM

- Bend your elbows and raise your forearms off the ground while performing this exercise. These movements reduce the lateral support that you provide to your body and make your core work harder.

Do not be alarmed if you find yourself corkscrewing off your mat. As your core strength improves, your body will be able to counter this tugging. While you are still building up that core strength, you can reduce resistance by bending your knees, which will increase your leverage when moving your legs.

FIRE HYDRANTS

MUSCLE TARGET: Glutes (medius)
EQUIPMENT: None

FORM

1
Get on your hands and knees on your exercise mat.

2
Keep your right knee bent and raise your right leg out toward the side as high as you can.

Complete your target number of reps, then switch to your other side.

ADVANCED FORM

- When working the right leg during this exercise, hold your left arm off the ground and extended in front of you. By removing one of the supports for your body, you introduce instability to the exercise. Switch arms and repeat on the other side.

Tip

In order to fully engage the gluteus medius, make sure that you do not rotate your body as you lift your leg. Keep your body square, and focus on moving nothing but your leg.

KICKBACKS

MUSCLE TARGET: Glutes
EQUIPMENT: None

REPS
20-30

FORM

1

Get on your hands and knees on your exercise mat. Bring your right knee in toward your chest.

2

Extend your right leg behind you as high as you can, then return it to the starting position. This constitutes 1 rep.

Complete your target number of reps, then switch to the other leg.

ADVANCED FORM

■ When working the right leg during this movement, hold your left arm off the ground and extended in front of you. Switch arms and repeat on the other side.

Tip

To get full extension, imagine that you are trying to kick a target behind you.

SUPERMANS

MUSCLE TARGETS: Lower back, glutes (maximus)

EQUIPMENT: Medicine ball or dumbbell (advanced)

FORM

1

Lie facedown on an exercise mat
with your arms outstretched.

2

Arch your body upward, raising your
shoulders and your legs simultaneously,
then lower back down. This constitutes
1 rep.

 Perform the reps quickly, as pulses rather
than as slow movements.

ADVANCED FORM

■ Hold a light weight in your outstretched arms while performing this movement.

COACH'S NOTE

This exercise involves a relatively limited range of motion, so don't be discouraged if you feel that you are not raising up high enough; you probably are.

V SIT-UPS

↘ **MUSCLE TARGETS:** Abs, hip flexors

EQUIPMENT: Medicine ball or dumbbell (advanced)

FORM

1

Sit on your exercise mat with your hands held by your sides and your legs extended straight in front of you.

2

Lean back and raise your legs off the ground.

3

Balance on your tailbone and raise your legs and torso up toward one another. Then lower your upper body and legs back down.

 This constitutes 1 rep.

ADVANCED FORM

■ Hold a weight in the air in front of you during this exercise.

Tip

Focus on pointing your heels. This helps you cue your body to keep your knees extended.

COACH'S NOTE

If you are having trouble balancing while performing this exercise, put your hands on the floor for stability.

LEG CROSSOVERS

MUSCLE TARGETS: Adductors, glutes (medius), abs, hip flexors, lower back

EQUIPMENT: None

REPS
10–20

FORM

1

Sit on your exercise mat with your legs outstretched in front of you and your hands behind you, bracing your upper body.

2

Keeping your legs straight, cross the left leg over the right, then swing them as wide apart as possible.

Bring your legs back together, though this time cross the right leg over the left. This constitutes 1 rep.

ADVANCED FORM

■ Raise your hands off the floor and hold them outstretched to your side while performing this movement. This leaves you balancing on your tailbone, which puts more stress on your core to keep you from toppling over.

JACKKNIVES

MUSCLE TARGETS: Abs, hip flexors
EQUIPMENT: Stability ball

FORM

1
Lie facedown on
your stability ball.

-------→

2
Roll your body forward until
you can put your palms
down on the floor and the
front of the ball is lined up
with your knees.

3
Raise your hips up in the air,
roll the ball forward, then
roll the ball back out as you
straighten out your body.

 This constitutes 1 rep.

ADVANCED FORM

- Hold your body in the raised position for a count of 5 before returning back to the floor.

Tip

Maintain proper form by imagining that there is a rope around your waist that is pulling you upward.

WINDSHIELD WIPERS

MUSCLE TARGETS: Obliques, hip flexors, abs (transverse)
EQUIPMENT: None

FORM

1

Lie faceup on your exercise mat, with your legs straight up in the air and your knees extended and locked. Place your arms outward, palms down.

2

Keep your legs together and swing them down to your right side as far as you can comfortably let them fall. Aim to keep your shoulders flat on the mat.

 Swing your legs in one smooth motion over to your left side, then return to the right side. This constitutes 1 rep.

ADVANCED FORM

■ Keep your arms in closer to your body while performing this movement. This removes some of the leverage your arms enjoy as they maintain lateral support to counterbalance the weight of your legs dropping to one side and then the other. This forces your arms and core to work harder to keep you from toppling over.

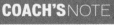

Tip

When you first do this exercise, keep your knees bent to reduce strain on your core. As you improve your strength, try to keep your legs straight. Performing this exercise may at first drag you off your mat, but that will stop as you begin to build the strength to hold your body in place.

COACH'S NOTE

This exercise is not only a good strengthening movement for your core; it is also a good stretch for the iliotibial band, a strip of connective tissue on the outside of your legs.

STABILITY BALL LEG CURLS

> ↘ **MUSCLE TARGET:** Hamstrings, abs (transverse), hip flexors
> **EQUIPMENT:** Stability ball

**# REPS
10–30**

FORM

1

Lie faceup on an exercise mat, with your heels on a stability ball. Raise your hips in the air, and hold a rigid line from your shoulders to your heels. Keep your arms on the floor at your sides to maintain balance.

2

Keeping your hips in the air, bend your knees and roll the ball inward toward your backside, then straighten your legs and roll the ball outward again.

 This constitutes 1 rep.

ADVANCED FORM

■ Perform this exercise while holding your arms in the air. This removes the lateral support that they provided when you had them on the floor at your sides, which makes your core work harder.

Tip

If necessary, spread your feet slightly on the ball to maintain stability.

KNEE TUCKS

 MUSCLE TARGETS: Hip flexors, abs (transverse)
EQUIPMENT: Stability ball

**# REPS
10-30**

FORM

1

Get into plank position, facing downward with your palms on the floor, your elbows extended, and your body held off the ground in a rigid line, with your feet resting on top of a stability ball.

2

Keeping your upper body steady, bend your knees and roll the ball inward toward you.

Once you are fully tucked, extend your legs again. This constitutes 1 rep.

ADVANCED FORM

■ Alternate **Knee Tucks** with **Push-Ups.** See the second Advanced Form option for Push-Ups, page 91.

Tip

Getting your feet on the ball may take a little finesse. One method is to get on all fours, with your knees on the ground and your feet on the ball behind you, holding it in place. Raise your body up while keeping your feet on the ball, and adjust as necessary once you have unfurled into a straight position.

4
THE
WORKOUTS

Getting in a random workout here and there is different from following a workout plan. Even though an individual workout might leave you feeling energized and eager for more, each workout in a structured plan moves you closer to your targeted short-term and long-term fitness goals, which is something that no single workout, or series of unconnected workouts, can accomplish.

A workout plan, then, is progressive in that each workout builds on the previous one and prepares you for the next one, like steps up a ladder. For us, this involves working on our themes of increasing core strength, improving balance, and developing better strength in the fundamental running motion from workout to workout and from week to week.

The progressive nature of our workout plan refers not just to the series of workouts, but also to each workout within the plan. The exercises here are not arranged haphazardly; they are stacked so as to first warm up the muscles we will be targeting within the workout and

The will to win means nothing
without the will to prepare.

JUMA IKANGAA
Tanzanian marathon champion and Olympian

then to allow some muscles to rest while others are being challenged. The exercises within each workout are arranged for effectiveness and for efficiency. As a result, many exercises transition easily into the next movement on the schedule.

Each week includes a summary of that week's goals, and each workout within that week has a statement of purpose. As you will see, we will be changing all the variables at our disposal during the course of this plan—including adding more exercises, adopting advanced forms of these exercises, and adding more sets and more reps—to continually increase the challenge we put on your body. In this way, we will trigger the adaptations we seek.

The exercises in Chapter 3 were organized into two basic categories: standing exercises and floor exercises. Following that division, the workout routines in this chapter are structured to flow naturally from one exercise to another when exercises from each group are placed back-to-back. This makes it easier and more efficient to move from one exercise to the next, as you will not need to repeatedly get up off the floor or lie down between exercises.

We also rotate between the muscle groups described earlier so that each muscle group worked gets some rest breaks while others are being exercised.

The end result of this organization is a faster, more effective workout that can be completed in 30 minutes or less.

Warming Up

Before you begin any workout, be sure to warm up. The workouts here do not involve lifting heavy weights or doing explosive movements, so the odds are low that you will injure a muscle or ligament even if you have not warmed up. Still, it is a good idea to make sure you are fully prepared for your workout with a little pre-exercise movement. Doing so will make your muscles and ligaments more pliable and release synovial fluid into your joints, which increases your range of motion, increases your comfort during the exercises, makes your workout more effective, and reduces the risk of injury.

A warm-up need not take much time. It may be as little as 10 minutes of continuous activity that raises your temperature and causes you to breathe harder and break a sweat. Running, cycling, and skipping rope are a few of the many options you might choose from.

The goal here is simply to raise your body temperature and signal to your nervous system that it is going to be called upon to work hard. But do not mistake the warm-up for an actual workout. Some people become a little too enthusiastic during the warm-up and begin to push harder for a longer period of time. This may be a mistake; adding intensity and duration to your warm-up can deplete your fuel stores and leave you feeling weak and uninspired when your strength workout begins. Don't

TO STRETCH OR NOT TO STRETCH BEFORE YOUR WORKOUT?

Some people like to stretch following their warm-up and before they begin exercising. But recent research indicates that stretching leaves you momentarily weaker than you were before, which compromises your ability to exercise closer to your true limits.

Why is this the case? Muscle strength comes from contractile power, which is stored under tension within each muscle cell. Think of your muscles as rubber bands: If they lose their elasticity, they lose the ability to snap back forcefully.

A stretch pushes the muscle and loosens it, just as age might do to a rubber band. Without that elastic rebound, the muscle is not able to generate as much force as it had just moments before. The result is a diminished ability to lift weights or do more reps, which means that your workout generates a lowered adaptation response and leads to less improvement in strength and fitness.

My recommendation? Save your stretching for after the workout, when your muscles are not being asked to do any more work.

make the mistake of leaving your day's best effort in the warm-up.

The warm-up serves one more purpose: It can help you shift psychologically from a physically passive phase to an active one. Strength training usually requires more focus than does running. In fact, running's effectiveness in providing an escape from directed thinking is one of its most appealing characteristics. But a distracted strength trainer runs the risk of inadvertently doing exercises incorrectly, which can result in injury.

The warm-up reduces this risk by providing a transition time for you to think about the upcoming workout as you gradually move from being sedentary to being active. Over time, your nervous system will even start to recognize the warm-up as a precursor of a hard strength workout, and it will automatically begin to dump adrenaline into your bloodstream to help you prepare.

For all of these reasons, don't give your warm-up short shrift, even when you are on a tight schedule.

WEEK 1

The goal of this week's workouts is to introduce you to many of the exercises and the exercise progressions we will be using in our workout. We will begin the process of building strength, but the central focus will be on establishing a solid foundation. With that in mind, make sure that you are clear about how each of the movements is to be performed before you attempt any of these exercises, reviewing the explanations in Chapter 3 as necessary, and that you are comfortable with each movement before going on to the next one.

CORE AND HIPS I (p. 135)

CORE AND UPPER-BODY DUMBBELL (p. 137)

CORE AND HIPS I

Purpose: This workout introduces you to exercises that strengthen your gluteus medius, which directly increases your lateral stability while running. Strengthening this muscle ultimately results in less strain on your iliotibial bands, hips, and knees.

The Workout

1.	Side Leg Raises (p. 104)		**10** reps each side
2.	Adductor Leg Raises (p. 108)		**10** reps each side
3.	Side Crunches (p. 102)		**15** reps each side
4.	Windshield Wipers (p. 124)		**10** reps
5.	Hip Raises (p. 88)		**20** reps
6.	Leg Raises (p. 100)		**10** reps
7.	Fire Hydrants (p. 112)		**12** reps each side

Continued

8.	Crunches (p. 92)		🔥 **15** reps
9.	Supermans (p. 116)		🔥 **15** reps
10.	Push-Ups (p. 90)		🔥 **10** reps, starting at knees or dropping to knees after a few reps if necessary

CORE AND UPPER-BODY DUMBBELL

Purpose: This workout introduces you to upper-body and core exercises that aim to strengthen your transverse abdominus, stabilize your hips and spine, and help generate twisting power. They also strengthen your arms, back, and shoulders. These exercises add weight resistance to your workout, which puts more pressure on your body, so be vigilant in demonstrating proper form.

The Workout

1.	Weighted Swings (p. 50)		**10** reps each side
2.	Torso Twists (p. 48)		**10** reps
3.	The Phoenix (p. 56)		**10** reps
4.	Crunches (p. 92)		**20** reps
5.	Deadlifts and Front Raises (p. 52)		**10** reps
6.	The Discus-Thrower (p. 60)		**10** reps each side

Continued

7.	Leg Raises (p. 100)		🔘 **14** reps
8.	Crossover Crunches (p. 94)		🔘 **20** reps
9.	Low Reverse Flyes (p. 82)		🔘 **10** reps
10.	Squats and Shoulder Presses (p. 58)		🔘 **12** reps

WEEK 2

The goal of this week's workouts is to improve balance. We introduce the exercises that require your body to learn how to hold itself still when unbalanced, which strengthens both the related muscle groups and their neural pathways.

For some people, these exercises may prove to be easy to master right from the start, but for others there may be a longer learning curve. Do not be discouraged if you have difficulty with these at first; you will get there soon enough.

Stand next to a wall or steady piece of furniture and reach out for a stabilizing touch when necessary. As you get stronger, you will find yourself reaching out for that support less often.

LATERAL BALANCE I (p. 140)

LEGS, UPPER BODY, AND CORE (p. 142)

LATERAL BALANCE I

Purpose: Working on balance through these exercises strengthens your proprioceptors and prepares your body for the instability of landing while running. By also working your hips, we help your body stay in proper alignment throughout the running motion. Many of the exercises in this workout challenge your sense of balance by requiring you to stand on one leg.

The Workout

1.	Front Leg Swings (p. 70)		**10** reps each side
2.	One-Legged Deadlifts (p. 54)		**10** reps each side
3.	Standing Hurdles (p. 72)		**10** reps each side
4.	Lateral Leg Swings (p. 68)		**10** reps each side
5.	Standing Reverse Hurdles (p. 74)		**10** reps each side
6.	Crunches (p. 92)		**20** reps

7.	Fire Hydrants (p. 112)		12 reps each side
8.	Kickbacks (p. 114)		12 reps each side
9.	Walking Lunges (p. 64)		2 sets (down and back, twice)

LEGS, UPPER BODY, AND CORE

Purpose: With this workout we introduce some of the key leg movements of this program, as well as continue to strengthen core muscle groups.

The Workout

1.	Knee Crunches (p. 96)		**10** reps
2.	Hip Raises (p. 88)		**30** reps
3.	Push-Ups (p. 90)		**15** reps, dropping to knees if necessary
4.	Side Crunches (p. 102)		**20** reps each side
5.	High Reverse Flyes (p. 80)		**10** reps
6.	Side Lunges (p. 66)		**10** reps
7.	Arm Circles (p. 62)		**10** reps

8.	Step-Ups (p. 76)		**10** reps each side
9.	Reverse Arm Circles (p. 62)		**10** reps
10.	Windshield Wipers (p. 124)		**10** reps
11.	Pullovers (p. 78)		**10** reps

WEEK 3

The goal of this week's workouts is building muscle endurance, which is the ability to sustain an intense effort for an extended period of time. We accomplish this by increasing the volume of the workout with repeated sets of some exercises.

DUMBBELLS AND CORE I (p. 145)

DUMBBELLS AND CORE II (p. 147)

DUMBBELLS AND CORE I

Purpose: In addition to building endurance, we return to dumbbell exercises in this workout as we continue to lay the foundation for future workouts.

The Workout

1.	Crunches (p. 92)		**15** reps
2.	Low Reverse Flyes (p. 82)		**12** reps
3.	Leg Raises (p. 100)		**10** reps
4.	High Reverse Flyes (p. 80)		**12** reps
5.	Crunches (p. 92)		**15** reps
6.	Leg Raises (p. 100)		**10** reps
7.	Dumbbell Chest Presses (p. 84)		**14** reps

Continued

8.	Supermans (p. 116)	20 reps
9.	Pullovers (p. 78)	12 reps
10.	Supermans (p. 116)	20 reps
11.	Squats and Shoulder Presses (p. 58)	14 reps
12.	Side Hip Raises (p. 106)	10 reps each side
13.	Kickbacks (p. 114)	20 reps

DUMBBELLS AND CORE II

Purpose: Here we continue to build muscle endurance by adding a second set to the dumbbell exercises we began with in Week 1 while continuing to do core exercises between each dumbbell set.

The Workout

1.	Windshield Wipers (p. 124)		**14** reps
2.	Weighted Swings (p. 50)		**12** reps each side
3.	Crossover Crunches (p. 94)		**20** reps
4.	The Discus-Thrower (p. 60)		**10** reps each side
5.	Torso Twists (p. 48)		**12** reps
6.	Knee Crunches (p. 96)		**20** reps
7.	Deadlifts and Front Raises (p. 52)		**12** reps

Continued

8.	Windshield Wipers (p. 124)		🕹 **14** reps
9.	Weighted Swings (p. 50)		🕹 **10** reps each side
10.	Crossover Crunches (p. 94)		🕹 **20** reps
11.	The Discus-Thrower (p. 60)		🕹 **12** reps each side
12.	Torso Twists (p. 48)		🕹 **10** reps
13.	Knee Crunches (p. 96)		🕹 **20** reps
14.	Deadlifts and Front Raises (p. 52)		🕹 **10** reps

WEEK 4

By now, your body has started to acclimate to
the new training program. We respond to these improvements
by raising the difficulty level slightly this week. We are also
introducing another piece of equipment: the stability ball.

This is a good time to check on your improvement by trying
the one-legged stand test described in the Introduction. Another
way to gauge improvement is to repeat the first workout from
Week 1 and compare your postworkout fatigue level then and now.

CORE AND HIPS II (p. 150)

LATERAL BALANCE II (p. 152)

CORE AND HIPS II

Purpose: This workout focuses on strengthening the stabilizing muscles of your core by increasing instability.

The Workout

1.	Push-Ups (p. 90)		Aim for **20** reps, dropping to knees if necessary
2.	Stability Ball Leg Curls (p. 126)		**10** reps
3.	Crunches *Advanced Form* (p. 93)		**20** reps
4.	Leg Raises *Advanced Form* (p. 101)		**15** reps
5.	Crunches *Advanced Form* (p. 93)		**15** reps
6.	Knee Tucks (p. 128)		**10** reps
7.	Hip Raises *Advanced Form* (p. 89)		**10** reps each side

8.	Side Crunches (p. 102)		**20** reps, right side
9.	Side Hip Raises (p. 106)		**10** reps, right side
10.	Side Crunches (p. 102)		**20** reps, left side
11.	Side Hip Raises (p. 106)		**10** reps, left side
12.	Push-Ups (p. 90)		As many as possible, at least **10** reps, even if from knees
13.	Side Crunches (p. 102)		**20** reps, right side
14.	Side Hip Raises (p. 106)		**10** reps, right side
15.	Side Crunches (p. 102)		**20** reps, left side
16.	Side Hip Raises (p. 106)		**10** reps, left side
17.	Fire Hydrants (p. 112)		**20** reps each side

LATERAL BALANCE II

Purpose: With this workout, we double the volume of standing hip exercises that we began with in Week 2 while continuing to work on improving upper-body strength and balance by incorporating dumbbell work.

The Workout

1.	Front Leg Swings (p. 70)		**12** reps each side
2.	High Reverse Flyes (p. 80)		**12** reps
3.	Lateral Leg Swings (p. 68)		**12** reps each side
4.	Low Reverse Flyes (p. 82)		**14** reps
5.	One-Legged Deadlifts (p. 54)		**12** reps each side
6.	Standing Hurdles (p. 72)		**12** reps each side
7.	Standing Reverse Hurdles (p. 74)		**12** reps each side

8.	Dumbbell Chest Presses (p. 84)		**14** reps
9.	Front Leg Swings (p. 70)		**12** reps each side
10.	Pullovers (p. 78)		**14** reps
11.	Lateral Leg Swings (p. 68)		**12** reps each side
12.	Deadlifts and Front Raises (p. 52)		**14** reps
13.	Standing Hurdles (p. 72)		**12** reps each side
14.	One-Legged Deadlifts (p. 54)		**12** reps each side
15.	Standing Reverse Hurdles (p. 74)		**12** reps each side

WEEK 5

This week's workouts introduce more advanced forms to the exercises and continue to build overall volume while building strength in the working muscles and stabilizers.

CORE AND HIPS III

Purpose: We continue to build lateral strength by working on the gluteus medius and stabilizer muscles, in addition to continuing work on the abs, chest, shoulders, and triceps.

The Workout

1.	Push-Ups (p. 90)		Aim for at least **20** reps (add 2 more if you can!)
2.	Hip Raises *Advanced Form* (p. 89)		**10** reps each side
3.	The Russian Twist (p. 98)		**20** reps
4.	Leg Raises *Advanced Form* (p. 101)		Aim for **10** reps, then **5** regular Leg Raises
5.	Side Crunches (p. 102)		**20** reps
6.	Side Leg Raises (p. 104)		**20** reps
7.	Adductor Leg Raises (p. 108)		**20** reps

Continued

8.	Side Hip Raises (p. 106)		**20** reps
9.	Push-Ups (p. 90)		**10** reps
10.	Leg Circles (p. 110)		**10** reps clockwise, then **10** reps counterclockwise
11.	Fire Hydrants *Advanced Form* (p. 113)		**20** reps each side
12.	Kickbacks *Advanced Form* (p. 115)		**20** reps each side
13.	Supermans (p. 116)		**20** reps
14.	Crunches *Advanced Form* (p. 93)		**10** reps
15.	Stability Ball Leg Curls (p. 126)		**20** reps
16.	Jackknives (p. 122)		**10** reps
17.	Push-Ups (p. 90)		As many as possible

CORE AND HIPS IV

Purpose: We have spent the past month building strength in our abs (the transverse abdominus, obliques, and rectus abdominus), so now we raise the bar by introducing new exercises as well as increasing the difficulty by adding more reps. At the same time, we are continuing to engage the upper body.

The Workout

1.	Torso Twists (p. 48)		**20** reps
2.	Weighted Swings (p. 50)		**20** reps
3.	The Russian Twist (p. 98)		**20** reps
4.	Deadlifts and Front Raises (p. 52)		**20** reps
5.	V Sit-Ups (p. 118)		**10** reps
6.	The Phoenix (p. 56)		**20** reps
7.	Squats and Shoulder Presses (p. 58)		**20** reps

Continued

8.	Crunches *Advanced Form* (p. 93)		**10** reps
9.	One-Legged Deadlifts (p. 54)		**20** reps each side
10.	Side Hip Raises (p. 106)		**20** reps each side
11.	The Discus-Thrower (p. 60)		**20** reps
12.	Side Crunches (p. 102)		**20** reps each side
13.	One-Legged Deadlifts (p. 54)		**20** reps each side
14.	Arm Circles (p. 62)		**20** reps
15.	Lateral Leg Swings (p. 68)		**20** reps each side
16.	Reverse Arm Circles (p. 62)		**20** reps
17.	Front Leg Swings (p. 70)		**20** reps each side

WEEK 6

This week we really step up our game by aiming to increase our volume and diversity of exercises. We divide our workouts into one weight-resistance workout and one body-weight workout. If you are comfortable with the base form of each workout, try a more advanced version, as suggested.

WEIGHT-RESISTANCE WORK

Purpose: This workout improves muscle strength and endurance by increasing the workload with dumbbells or the medicine ball, building on what we have already accomplished by adding to the total volume. In this workout we stack different exercises together to work particular muscle groups, such as the chest or the shoulders. And as always, we add in core work.

This workout asks you to do a group of similar exercises, performing a high number of repetitions of each, while mixing in abdominal work to give the upper body a rest. We then run through all the weighted exercises again, but back-to-back, dropping down to fewer repetitions of each.

The Workout

1.	High Reverse Flyes (p. 80)		**20** reps
2.	Low Reverse Flyes (p. 82)		**20** reps
3.	Crunches (p. 92)		**20** reps
4.	The Phoenix (p. 56)		**14** reps
5.	Deadlifts and Front Raises (p. 52)		**14** reps

6.	Crunches (p. 92)		⌇ **20** reps
7.	The Discus-Thrower (p. 60)		⌇ **14** reps
8.	Weighted Swings (p. 50)		⌇ **14** reps each side
9.	Leg Raises (p. 100)		⌇ **14** reps
10.	Dumbbell Chest Presses *Advanced Form* (p. 85)		⌇ **20** reps
11.	Pullovers *Advanced Form* (p. 79)		⌇ **20** reps
12.	Leg Raises (p. 100)		⌇ **14** reps
13.	High Reverse Flyes (p. 80)		⌇ **10** reps
14.	Low Reverse Flyes (p. 82)		⌇ **20** reps
15.	The Phoenix (p. 56)		⌇ **10** reps

Continued

16.	Deadlifts and Front Raises (p. 52)		✎ **10** reps
17.	The Discus-Thrower (p. 60)		✎ **10** reps each side
18.	Dumbbell Chest Presses *Advanced Form* (p. 85)		✎ **10** reps
19.	Pullovers *Advanced Form* (p. 79)		✎ **10** reps

WORKOUT 12

TOTAL CORE

Purpose: This workout includes body-weight exercises only, focusing on all the muscles of the core. Our aim is to do a large variety of movements in order to work the many core muscles in several different ways.

The Workout

1.	Walking Lunges *Advanced Form* (p. 65)		⌖ **20** paces out, then back
2.	Push-Ups (p. 90)		⌖ Aim for **25** reps, dropping to knees if necessary
3.	Leg Crossovers (p. 120)		⌖ **20** reps
4.	Stability Ball Leg Curls (p. 126)		⌖ **10** reps
5.	Crunches *Advanced Form* (p. 93)		⌖ **30** reps
6.	Leg Raises (p. 100)		⌖ **15** reps
7.	Jackknives (p. 122)		⌖ **10** reps

Continued

8.	Knee Tucks (p. 128)		**10** reps
9.	Supermans (p. 116)		**20** reps
10.	Hip Raises *Advanced Form* (p. 89)		**10** reps each side
11.	Leg Circles (p. 110)		**10** reps clockwise, then **10** reps counterclockwise
12.	Side Hip Raises (p. 106)		**20** reps each side
13.	Fire Hydrants *Advanced Form* (p. 113)		**20** reps each side
14.	Kickbacks *Advanced Form* (p. 114)		**20** reps each side
15.	Side Crunches (p. 102)		**20** reps each side
16.	Step-Ups (p. 76)		**10** reps each side
17.	Side Lunges (p. 66)		**14** reps

18.	Lateral Leg Swings (p. 68)		20 reps each side
19.	Front Leg Swings (p. 70)		20 reps each side
20.	Standing Hurdles (p. 72)		20 reps each side
21.	Standing Reverse Hurdles (p. 74)		20 reps each side

WEEK 7

By now we are familiar with all the exercises in our arsenal, so this week we are going to focus on doing the advanced form of these exercises.

Do not worry if you cannot hit the target number of repetitions in the advanced form; do what you can, practicing perfect form, then drop back down to the basic form for the remainder of the set if necessary.

LATERAL BALANCE III

Purpose: This workout stresses your lateral stabilizers, which include your gluteus medius and your transverse abdominus.

The Workout

1.	Torso Twists (p. 48)		**20** reps
2.	The Russian Twist (p. 98)		**20** reps
3.	Crossover Crunches (p. 94)		**30** reps
4.	Side Hip Raises (p. 106)		**20** reps
5.	Side Crunches (p. 102)		**30** reps
6.	Side Leg Raises *Advanced Form* (p. 105)		**20** reps
7.	Supermans (p. 116)		**30** reps

Continued

8.	Side Lunges (p. 66)		**20** reps
9.	Standing Hurdles (p. 72)		**20** reps
10.	Standing Reverse Hurdles (p. 74)		**20** reps
11.	One-Legged Deadlifts (p. 54)		**20** reps each side
12.	Torso Twists (p. 48)		**20** reps
13.	The Russian Twist (p. 98)		**20** reps
14.	Crossover Crunches (p. 94)		**30** reps
15.	Side Hip Raises (p. 106)		**20** reps
16.	Side Crunches (p. 102)		**30** reps
17.	Side Leg Raises *Advanced Form* (p. 105)		**20** reps

18.	Supermans (p. 116)		**30** reps
19.	Side Lunges (p. 66)		**20** reps
20.	Standing Hurdles (p. 72)		**20** reps
21.	Standing Reverse Hurdles (p. 74)		**20** reps
22.	One-Legged Deadlifts (p. 54)		**20** reps each side

UPPER BODY AND ABS

Purpose: We focused on your stabilizers in our last workout. Here we work the upper body and rectus abdominus.

The Workout

1.	Dumbbell Chest Press-es *Advanced Form* (p. 85)		**20** reps
2.	Crunches *Advanced Form* (p. 93)		**20** reps
3.	Low Reverse Flyes (p. 82)		**20** reps
4.	Crunches (p. 92)		**35** reps
5.	Dumbbell Chest Press-es *Advanced Form* (p. 85)		**20** reps
6.	Crunches *Advanced Form* (p. 93)		**20** reps
7.	High Reverse Flyes (p. 80)		**20** reps

8.	Crunches (p. 92)		**35** reps
9.	Deadlifts and Front Raises (p. 52)		**20** reps
10.	Leg Raises (p. 100)		**20** reps
11.	Knee Crunches (p. 96)		**20** reps
12.	Deadlifts and Front Raises (p. 52)		**20** reps
13.	Leg Raises (p. 100)		**20** reps
14.	Knee Crunches (p. 96)		**20** reps
15.	The Phoenix (p. 56)		**20** reps
16.	Crossover Crunches (p. 94)		**30** reps

Continued

17.	The Phoenix (p. 56)		**20** reps
18.	Crossover Crunches (p. 94)		**30** reps

WEEK 8

For this final week of our program, we test your body by organizing the workouts in a new way. This provides a brand-new training stimulus to your body, just when it was getting used to the regular routine. This change triggers a new adaptation response.

1-SET WORKOUT

Purpose: With this workout we aim to improve muscle endurance by quickly moving from one exercise to the next with little or no rest time between sets. Even though we have been adding a second set to each exercise in many of our recent workouts, we change things up in this session by doing only 1 set of each exercise, but we cover more ground by adding in a greater variety of exercises.

The Workout

1.	Torso Twists (p. 48)		**20** reps
2.	Side Lunges (p. 66)		**20** reps
3.	Weighted Swings (p. 50)		**10** reps each side
4.	Lateral Leg Swings (p. 68)		**20** reps each side
5.	Deadlifts and Front Raises (p. 52)		**20** reps
6.	Front Leg Swings (p. 70)		**20** reps each side

7.	Squats and Shoulder Presses (p. 58)		**20** reps
8.	The Discus-Thrower (p. 60)		**14** reps each side
9.	Standing Hurdles (p. 72)		**20** reps each side
10.	Low Reverse Flyes (p. 82)		**20** reps
11.	Standing Reverse Hurdles (p. 74)		**20** reps each side
12.	High Reverse Flyes (p. 80)		**20** reps, one arm at a time, separately
13.	Hip Raises (p. 88)		**30** reps
14.	Crossover Crunches (p. 94)		**20** reps each side
15.	Dumbbell Chest Presses *Advanced Form* (p. 85)		**20** reps each side
16.	Pullovers (p. 78)		**20** reps

Continued

17.	Knee Crunches (p. 96)		30 reps
18.	The Russian Twist (p. 98)		20 reps
19.	Stability Ball Leg Curls (p. 126)		20 reps
20.	Windshield Wipers (p. 124)		20 reps

WORKOUT + SINGLE EXERCISE FOCUS

Purpose: We are going to continue shaking things up and giving the body something new to deal with in this workout by returning to one exercise in particular—the Push-Up—again and again between sets of other exercises. Although each set of Push-Ups has fewer repetitions than you have done up to now, the total volume is greater than your body has yet experienced. This may leave you a bit sore for a day or two, but that just signals that an adaption is taking place.

Keep in mind that, although the Push-Up is a central, foundational type of strength-building exercise, this basic format works with any exercise. Create your own variations of this routine by choosing a single exercise to repeat again and again during the course of the workout.

Along with the Push-Ups is the familiar assortment of core work and other exercises that you have come to know over the past weeks.

The Workout

1.	Push-Ups (p. 90)		**10** reps
2.	Hip Raises (p. 88)		**30** reps
3.	Crunches (p. 92)		**30** reps
4.	Push-Ups (p. 90)		**10** reps

Continued

5.	Crossover Crunches (p. 94)		✏ **25** reps each side
6.	Knee Crunches (p. 96)		✏ **30** reps
7.	Push-Ups (p. 90)		✏ **10** reps
8.	Leg Raises (p. 100)		✏ **20** reps
9.	Side Crunches (p. 102)		✏ **20** reps each side
10.	Push-Ups (p. 90)		✏ **10** reps
11.	Side Leg Raises (p. 104)		✏ **20** reps each side
12.	Adductor Leg Raises (p. 108)		✏ **20** reps each side
13.	Push-Ups (p. 90)		✏ **10** reps
14.	Side Hip Raises (p. 106)		✏ **20** reps each side

15.	Push-Ups (p. 90)		10 reps
16.	Leg Circles (p. 110)		10 reps clockwise, then 10 reps counterclockwise
17.	Supermans (p. 116)		30 reps
18.	Push-Ups (p. 90)		10 reps
19.	Crunches *Advanced Form* (p. 93)		20 reps
20.	Windshield Wipers (p. 124)		20 reps
21.	Push-Ups (p. 90)		10 reps, or as many as you can possibly muster
22.	High Reverse Flyes (p. 80)		10 reps
23.	Low Reverse Flyes (p. 82)		10 reps
24.	Push-Ups (p. 90)		10 reps, or as many as you can possibly muster

If you really want to do
something, you'll find a way.
If you don't, you'll find an excuse.

JIM ROHN
Author and speaker

5
TAKING IT
ON THE ROAD

When we began this discussion, I promised you that this was a workout plan that you could implement right in your own home. And you can. However, when necessity or opportunity takes you to other places, you can still stay on track with your plan and effectively challenge your body in new and different ways.

In a Hotel

Many hotels have a dedicated exercise space for guests. Some-times, these hotel gyms contain the same pieces of equipment that we use in our routines, such as dumbbells and a BOSU. When that is the case during any of your travels, you can simply continue on your program without any breaks or modifications.

In those instances, however, when your hotel provides you nothing but a room, there is no need to despair. With a little creativity and improvisation, you can easily stay on track with your workout schedule.

First, prepare your workout space. Find a spot in the room with the greatest amount of open floor space, and if possible, clear away any light furniture that could get in your way. In a double room, this might just be the space between the beds.

Second, spread a bath towel on the floor. This will not only provide you with a bit more padding, but it will also help out with hygiene.

Third, target those exercises that do not require any more equipment than your own body. Fortunately, the program in this book contains a large number of purely body-weight exercises. Floor routines and standing balance routines are both fair game for your hotel workout, space permitting.

Fourth, if you would still like to use weights, head out to a nearby supermarket or sundry store and buy water in these denominations: two 20-ounce bottles, two 1-quart containers, and a single 1-gallon jug. Together, these will make up a rudimentary weight set that is cheap, effective, and recyclable.

Now you are set to work out. What is the best way to organize your workout? As we discussed in the Introduction, the best improvements from strength training—not just in improved muscle strength, but also in increased cardiovascular fitness—

come when the muscles are worked to fatigue or temporary failure. When you are working out at home and have access to all your equipment, that is not hard to achieve, but when you do not have access to your equipment, you will have to work more strategically to achieve the same effect. Here is what you will need to do:

■ **Wear out smaller supporting muscles before targeting the larger muscles.**
The usual strength training formula is to make sure that the big muscle groups get worked before the smaller ones so that fatigue in the small muscles does not limit what the larger ones can do, but on the road you will want to flip this formula because you will not have the equipment to fatigue the larger ones. In that case, tiring out the smaller ones first will help bring temporary muscle failure sooner. For example, do The Phoenix with your water bottles before you do Shoulder Presses, or do Biceps Curls with the water bottles before doing Low Reverse Flyes.*

■ **Focus on body-weight exercises before using improvised equipment.**
Similarly, your relatively light "water-bottle weights" will seem heavier

---

* The Biceps Curl is not an exercise that we targeted in our at-home workout, but it is simple to do: Holding a water bottle in each hand, bend your elbows simultaneously and raise the dumbbells up toward your shoulders. Be careful not to swing your body to raise the weight.

and more effective if your muscles are already tired before you pick the weights up. An example of this kind of progression would be to do Step-Ups before doing Squats while holding the water jug or to do Push-Ups before water-bottle Shoulder Presses.

■ **Create a circuit that will leave the muscles without a chance to rest and recover.** For a limited but effective workout, choose a small number of exercises and do them in quick succession several times in a row to achieve temporary muscles failure. An example would be to do 20 reps each of Squats, Push-Ups, Supermans, and Crunches in quick succession, then repeat 4 times. This workout takes 10 minutes or less, but it works the chest, shoulders, arms, legs, and lower back. That is a pretty impressive impact for such a limited workout.

■ **Try a new challenge.** When young boxer Larry Holmes hurt his right hand in training, he decided not to be depressed about what he could not do, and instead focused on perfecting his left jab while he gave his right hand a chance to heal. His improved left jab eventually carried him all the way to the world heavyweight championship. Take a lesson from Larry Holmes and make the best of what you can do when you are on the road. Aim to break your personal record for a bodyweight exercise—do more Push-Ups, Crunches, or Supermans than ever before.

If you will be away from home for more than one night, vary the exercises that you perform in order to avoid boredom. And remember that even if you do not feel as though you have got as good a workout as you usually get at home, a little is much better than none at all.

More than just providing maintenance work for your muscles, a hotel workout also serves another purpose: It helps keep you on a schedule. As you probably know from your running, momentum is a powerful force—in either direction. Action, or *in*action, tends to breed more of the same. Staying in a routine helps you stay on track.

WORKOUT 1

A Floor Workout

1.	**Push-Ups**	**10-20** reps
2.	**Side Leg Raises**	**20** reps, right side
3.	**Side Hip Raises**	**20** reps, right side
4.	**Crossover Crunches**	**30** reps, right side
5.	**Hip Raises**	**30** reps
6.	**Leg Raises**	**20** reps
7.	**Crossover Crunches**	**30** reps, left side
8.	**Side Hip Raises**	**20** reps, left side
9.	**Side Leg Raises**	**20** reps, left side

Repeat this entire sequence and end with 1 final set of Push-Ups, for a total of 3 sets of Push-Ups.

WORKOUT 2

A Water-Bottle Workout

1.	The Phoenix	**14** reps
2.	Deadlifts and Front Raises	**14** reps
3.	High Reverse Flyes	**14** reps
4.	Squats and Shoulder Presses	**14** reps
5.	Low Reverse Flyes	**14** reps
6.	Weighted Swings	**14** reps each side
7.	Torso Twists	**20** reps

Perform each exercise while holding a water bottle in each hand or with both hands, depending on the exercise. Repeat the sequence one or two times.

WORKOUT 3

A Mixed Standing Workout

1.	Standing Hurdles	**20** reps, right side
2.	Standing Reverse Hurdles	**20** reps, right side
3.	Lateral Leg Swings	**20** reps, right side
4.	Deadlifts and Front Raises	**20** reps
5.	Standing Hurdles	**20** reps, left side
6.	Standing Reverse Hurdles	**20** reps, left side
7.	Lateral Leg Swings	**20** reps, left side
8.	Side Lunges	**10** reps each side
9.	Torso Twists	**20** reps

Repeat sequence.

At the Gym

If you already belong to a gym, you should have no problem staying on track with your strength-building workout schedule. Most modern fitness facilities are more than just barbells and dumbbells these days; you should be able to find a range of balance boards and stability balls, as well as medicine balls of various sizes and weights.

But what about all the other equipment available at the gym?

Most good gyms have an extensive line-up of weight lifting stations that target every major muscle group in your body. Many people do all their workouts on these machines, either rotating from machine to machine in a circuit or doing several sets on a single machine before moving on to the next station.

I have no problem with those workouts. People who follow those routines are building and maintaining muscle mass and bone density, two of the main benefits of strength training, and they are doing so in a safe manner. There is a saying in fitness: The best exercise is the one that you will keep doing. Put another way, any movement that is not causing unnecessary strain is movement that you should keep doing.

Still, those machines are not getting you the kind of running-specific fitness that your effort deserves. So to make the most of your time in the gym, you should be doing things a little differently.

First, where possible, get your core more engaged by using one hand at time to do an exercise rather than both. On a chest press station, for example, do 14 reps using only your right hand, followed by 14 reps with your left. Similarly, you could use a rowing machine the same way or a shoulder press machine. By doing these exercises unilaterally rather than bilaterally, you will create some lateral pull on your body, even if you are sitting down, and this will force your core to get at least marginally more engaged.

Second, make use of the cable station. Used properly, this equipment fits very well into your routine. The key is to get your entire body turning to pull or push the cable handle. If you can succeed in that, you will be working your legs, hips, abs, and upper body, all in the same exercise.

Here is an example of what this kind of cable exercise looks like:

- Stand facing the cable machine, and set the handle height just above eye level.

- With your left foot forward and your right foot back, grab the handle with your right hand.

- Pull the handle toward your side, twisting your body as you pull. Your power should come from the rotation of your hips, not from your right arm.

- Unwind and return the handle to the starting position. This constitutes 1 rep.

- When you have completed your goal number of reps, reverse your stance and continue on the other side.

A similar movement would be to use this same format to *push* the handle:

- Stand with your back to the cable, with your left foot forward and your right foot back.

- Grip the handle with your right hand, holding it at shoulder level, with your right forearm parallel to the ground.

- Throw a controlled punch with the right hand, twisting your body as you reach forward.

- Return to the starting position. This constitutes 1 rep.

- Complete your goal number of reps, and switch to the other side.

The rotational movement of both these exercises is a common denominator in many sports. From baseball to golf and tennis, power is derived from engagement of the core and rotation of the hips.

Many more exercises can be performed on the cable machine, but please take this recommendation to heart: If you are going to experiment in a gym with new exercises, consider hiring a trainer to show you the proper way to perform them. We have spent a lot of time here talking about how to safely and effectively do our workouts at home and on the road. The same goes at the gym: If you are not sure how to use a piece of equipment in a gym, do not use it until a qualified staff member tells you how.

WORKOUT 4

A Sample Cable Workout

1.	**Twisting Cable Pulls**	**20** reps, right hand
2.	**Twisting Cable Pulls**	**20** reps, left hand
3.	**Twisting Cable Pulls** (a little heavier, perhaps 1 increment of weight more)	**14** reps, right hand
4.	**Twisting Cable Pulls** (a little heavier)	**14** reps, left hand
5.	**Cable Punches**	**20** reps, right hand
6.	**Cable Punches**	**20** reps, left hand
7.	**Cable Punches** (a little heavier)	**14** reps, right hand
8.	**Cable Punches** (a little heavier)	**14** reps, left hand

Incorporate this into a workout containing our other exercises.

6

A LIFETIME
OF FITNESS

The program presented here is a targeted routine designed to give you noticeable results in a set time frame. If you follow this program for 8 consecutive weeks, you will see improved strength, balance, and muscle endurance. If you do so with a goal race in mind at the end, you will have put yourself in a position to run stronger and more efficiently on that target day. But what then? What is supposed to come next?

Next Steps

Training cycles end, but training should not. The conclusion of our 8-week program does not signal the end of your strength training any more than the end of a road trip signals the perfect time to abandon your car. Having secured your hard-won strength gains, you are probably very interested in keeping them, and so you should. Simply enter into another 8-week cycle of training.

Physical fitness is not only one
of the most important keys to
a healthy body, it is the basis
of dynamic and creative
intellectual activity.

JOHN F. KENNEDY

If, however, you are interested in not just maintaining the strength you earned, but also in continuing to improve, then you need to continue challenging your body. Here are some suggestions on how to do so.

Mix Things Up

In the pages of this book you have been introduced to 40 different exercises and several advanced variations. The workouts are organized to focus on different training modes (body weight, balance, and weight resistance) and muscle groups (hips, abdominals, back, chest, and shoulders), but you should feel free to experiment among the nearly endless list of possible combinations. As long as your form is good, you can be as creative as you dare to be. With each new combination, you are giving your body a new challenge to adapt to, which leads to further increases in strength and improvements in neural pathways.

Add Volume

During the course of the 8-week program, we introduced more and more exercises into our repertoire and increased the overall volume of sets and repetitions until we more than doubled our workout load. In this same fashion, you can continue adding more exercises, sets, and reps to your workout, which spurs on greater strength

and muscle endurance gains.

Of course, this particular trend cannot continue indefinitely. There comes a point when adding more exercises does not lead to further improvements. In economics, this phenomenon is called "the Law of Diminishing Returns." It states that where a little may be good, and a little more may be better, a lot more may not be even better; in fact, it may actually be much worse.

Think of having a serving of your favorite dessert. That probably sounds wonderful. Two or even three servings may still sound pretty good, but having five or six servings starts to sound awful and even sickening.

The same is true of exercise. To spot when enough is too much, check your mood. One harbinger of physical burnout is a loss of interest in your workouts. If you are bored or feel burned out, that may be an indicator that your body needs a break.

Give your body needed rest by taking a few days off or by slipping in a week of lower-volume efforts in which you do fewer reps and fewer sets. Cutting the workout short like this will feel almost like a vacation. Enjoy it without guilt. Even though you will not make any improvements during this time, you will not have any appreciable loss in fitness either, and you will come roaring back with renewed enthusiasm after the fitness vacation ends.

Increase Difficulty

Each of the exercises introduced here is presented along with one or more variations. If you have not yet tried all these variations, you can structure future workouts around mastering these alternatives. Or you can challenge yourself by trying to create other, new variations, following these guidelines:

- **Keep it safe:** Try the exercise with little or no weights at first, and as always, ensure that you are properly warmed up beforehand.

- **Destabilize yourself:** Engage your core more by forcing it to work at balancing you. Sit on a stability ball, stand on a BOSU, or stand on one leg; do what it takes to add some wobble to your workout.

- **Involve more muscle groups and joints:** Make the exercise as complex as possible to make it as effective as possible.

Staying Healthy

Whenever we work out, whether with a strength training routine, a run, a bike ride, a swim, or any other mode that challenges us physically, the dynamics are essentially the same: If the challenge presented is well within the body's capability, then no change will occur, but if the challenge is a bit more than the body is acclimated to, then the workout will trigger an adaptation response and the body will resculpt itself to meet that challenge more effectively in the future. If, however, the training stimulus is greater than the body's ability to adapt—that is, we ask more of the body than it can reasonably handle—then the body breaks down. The result is injury.

It would be easy to say that if you are careful, you can always avoid injuries, but that is simply not the truth. Athletes at all levels, from weekend warriors to Olympians and world record holders, occasionally get on the wrong side of this calculation. The key is to avoid letting a little injury turn into a major layoff. How? By quickly and honestly assessing a possible injury and reacting appropriately and quickly.

Recognize When a Possible Problem Has Arisen

A bit of muscle soreness is to be expected after a hard workout and in some sense is even to be welcomed. As discussed, soreness indicates that a muscle group has been pushed beyond its comfort zone, which is a good thing.

But soreness is not to be confused with pain. If you experience a sharp pain in any muscle or joint, or if the soreness you feel does not abate after a few days, that is a warning sign. Do not wait for the pain to become worse. Call what you are experiencing an injury, accept that fact, and take charge of the situation.

Do Not Ignore the Problem

I am not a doctor, and you may not be either. Nonetheless, most of us are quite familiar with our own bodies. Combine that with some knowledge of past injury history and a bit of common sense, and it is not hard for us to put together a quick treatment plan. This plan should include the following:

- **Rest.** If something hurts, leave it alone. This advice may seem obvious, but too many runners—myself included— keep testing a painful muscle or joint even after it has become clear that something is very wrong there. Perhaps it is denial of the problem, or a hope that all that is necessary is to "walk it off," but whatever the reason, be smarter than you are brave. Lay off.

- **Ice.** Ice is still the best tool for treating inflammation. It is cheap and effective, and it does not have any of the bad side effects that anti-inflammatory drugs may have. Ice the affected area for 10 minutes, then take a 5-minute rest, repeating as necessary.

Assess How Serious the Problem Might Be

Self-help is a great way to treat an injury, but at some point the old saying holds true: A doctor who treats himself has a fool for a patient. If the soreness and pain that you are treating with rest and ice do not abate after several days, visit a doctor, preferably a sports doctor. The goal is to prevent a small injury from becoming a larger one, so the sooner you get the correct treatment for your problem, the better your odds are of being back out on the road running without pain.

The Longer View

The goal of this book is to improve your running by adding strength training to your routine. Although improved running form will certainly result from following this routine, the benefits of strength training are more far reaching than we have yet discussed.

According to the Centers for Disease Control and Prevention (CDC) Web page on physical activity, regular strength training brings a host of benefits, all of which become increasingly important as we age.

Arthritis Relief: Strength training has been shown to decrease pain experienced by test subjects with arthritis as effectively as medications, improve their physical performance, and reduce the symptoms of the disease. These benefits accrue to people with rheumatoid arthritis as well as osteoarthritis.*

Improved Balance: As we age, we become more susceptible to loss of balance, often resulting in falls that can cause bone fractures, which in some cases can lead to disabilities and even fatal complications. Strength training, especially when incorporating balancing movements, can reduce the incidence of falls by as much as 40 percent in the elderly, and as reduce the severity of those falls that do occur.

Increased Bone Density: We all are at risk for losing bone density as we age, but women in particular need to be aware of the danger of osteoporosis. Postmenopausal women can lose 1-2 percent of their bone mass annually. One study concluded that strength training increases bone density and reduces the risk for fractures among women aged 50-70.†

Proper Weight Maintenance: Although the program we have outlined here does not focus on adding lots of additional muscle, it is likely that your body com-

position will still change somewhat over the course of the 8-week training cycle. Because muscle tissue needs to be fed even when at rest, this change will result in an increased metabolism of up to 15 percent or more over the pretraining level.

Running, in contrast, burns more calories during exercise than does strength training, but it does not result in the same kind of ongoing rise in your resting metabolism.

Lower Risk of Diabetes: The CDC Web page reports that more than 14 million Americans now have type II diabetes, which is a staggering 300 percent increase over the past 40 years. Here is more bad news: These numbers are expected to get worse before they get better.

Diabetes increases the risk for heart and renal disease and is also the leading cause of blindness in older adults. Sadly, this disease, once associated with older adults, in increasingly appearing in teenagers and young adults.

The good news is that lifestyle changes—including engaging in strength training—can help older adults manage their diabetes as well as diabetes medication can.

---

* K. R. Baker et al., "The Efficacy of Home-Based Progressive Strength Training in Older Adults with Knee Osteoarthritis: A Randomized Controlled Trial," *Journal of Rheumatology* 28(7) (July 2001): 1655–1665.

† M. E. Nelson et al., "Effects of High-Intensity Strength Training on Multiple Risk Factors for Osteoporotic Fractures—A Randomized Controlled Trial," *JAMA* 24(272) (1994): 1909–1914.

Improved State of Mind: Strength training has been found in many cases to be as effective as prescribed medication in treating clinical depression. Although some of this impact might be due as much to a more positive outlook from improved health as it might be due to any changes in the brain chemistry involved in depression, strength training has nonetheless been shown to have a strong impact on the overall quality of life of those studied.[*]

Improved Sleep: People who engage in regular strength training fall asleep more quickly, sleep more deeply, awaken less often, and sleep longer.[†] These benefits are equal to those delivered by medication, but, as the CDC notes, without the side effects or the expense.

This is especially important for runners and other athletes, as human growth hormone, which is crucial to the recovery and healing process that follows training and racing, is released during sleep.

Reduced Risk of Heart Disease: Strength training has been found to increase aerobic capacity among cardiac patients who engaged in it three times a week. This finding compelled the American Heart Association to recommend strength training for patients in cardiac rehabilitation programs.

All these benefits can come from just 2-3 workouts a week. And even though running can deliver some of these same benefits, such as lowering the risk of heart disease and reducing the effects of depression, it cannot deliver all of them. Taken together, running and strength training provide a complementary blend of health-extending exercises, not just to make you a better runner, but also to keep you healthy and strong for as long as possible.

The Last Word

When we began this discussion, the main purpose of the book was understood to be better running, not a new focus on strength training. It was to be a tool for you to use to improve your running. Running would always come first.

I do not have any problem with any of that. For many of us, running is so deeply

---

[*] L. Lynette, L. L. Craft, and F. Perna, "The Benefits of Exercise for the Clinically Depressed," *Primary Care Companion to the Journal of Clinical Psychiatry* 6(3) (2004): 104–111.

[†] It has long been believed that engaging in exercise, while promoting sleep generally, may inhibit sleep if performed within an hour or two of bedtime. New studies indicate that this may not be true. To be on the safe side, try to do your workout at least an hour or two before you hit the sack. F. Togo et al., "Sleep Is Not Disrupted by Exercise in Patients with Chronic Fatigue Syndrome," *Medicine and Science in Sports and Exercise* 42(1) (January 2010): 16–22; S. D. Youngstedt et al., "The Effects of Acute Exercise on Sleep: A Quantitative Synthesis," *Sleep: Journal of Sleep Research and Sleep Medicine* 20(3) (March 1997): 203–214.

connected with our lives that it would be difficult, if not impossible, to separate the two. Sometimes it takes center stage, as on race day, and other times it plays a background role. But all thoughts and actions somehow touch upon running sooner or later.

Despite this, I am going to ask you to think of strength training not just as a means to an end, but also as an end in itself. Be open to the possibility that you may come to appreciate, and even enjoy, strength training for its own sake, just as you do running.

This will not make your workouts more effective; your muscles do not need you to be emotionally engaged in order to respond to strength training. But if you come to feel that strength training can enrich your life in ways that running cannot, you will enjoy these workouts more, which in turn will make you more likely to train consistently.

What we are going to talk about next does not involve more studies and charts or facts and figures. It is not about science at all. Instead, it is about your relationship to your body, the ways in which you experience it, and how strength training amplifies that experience.

TRUTH: Strength training creates increased body awareness.

When you work on specific muscles, you develop biofeedback loops, which is a fancy way of saying that you can feel more clearly how those muscles move and contract. This allows you to use your body more effectively, just as knowing how the parts of your car work and can be used will make you a better driver and make you more aware when something does not sound or feel right. Knowing your body in this way can enable you to quickly sense when adjustments in body position or movements need to be made or when an injury might occur.

TRUTH: Strength training makes living in your body more fun.

Earlier we reviewed the ways in which the different parts of the body interact to support each other—and cases in which this did not occur. When all the major muscle groups are working properly and shouldering their load, the result is a general feeling of power and good health. You can move smoothly, without being limited by a weak lower back or balance issues.

TRUTH: Strength training can be uniquely satisfying.

Running farther and faster can be enormously rewarding, but when it comes to delivering a sense of satisfaction and accomplishment, strength training has its value. The muscle fatigue that follows a good strength workout can create a deep sense of wellness, and the visible improvements that flow from even just a few weeks of dedicated training can be very satisfying.

TRUTH: *Strength training can take you to new places.*

Once you have achieved greater overall strength and fitness, you should have the confidence to attempt any new adventure that interests you. Whether it is stand-up paddle boarding, rock climbing, or kayaking, you will find that your new body needs a shorter learning curve to master a new physical challenge. Indeed, you can think of the fitness that you build by working your way through the exercises in this book as preparing you not just for better running, but also for a better, more active life.

And that, more than anything, should be the real goal of all your training. Treat your life as an adventure, on the roads, on the trails, and wherever your imagination may take you.

ABOUT THE AUTHOR

JEFF HOROWITZ ran his first marathon in 1987 and fell in love with the sport. Since then, he has run more than 170 marathons and ultramarathons around the world, from Antarctica to Africa and Asia, and at least one in every U.S. state.

Formerly a practicing attorney, Jeff quit law to help teach adults and at-risk youth how to lead healthier lifestyles, and to share his passion for running. He is a certified personal trainer and running, cycling, and triathlon coach (AFAA, USAT, USATF, USA Cycling, and RRCA).

Jeff is a former regional editor for *Competitor* magazine and is a frequent contributor to several running and fitness magazines. This is his third book; he previously released *My First 100 Marathons* and *Smart Marathon Training*.

Jeff is married to artist Stephanie Kay, with whom he has an 8-year-old son, Alex Michael.